CHOICES

Go Book GA

Rigby • Saxon • Steck-Vaughn

www.HarcourtAchieve.com
1.800.531.5015

Acknowledgements

Director of eLearning: Irwin F. Harris
Editor: Carol Alexander
Associate Design Director: Joyce Spicer
Senior Designer: Jim Cauthron
Photo Researcher: Nicole Mlakar
Editorial Development: Inkwell Publishing Solutions, Inc.
Photo credits: Photography by Photos.com Royalty Free,
Photodisc/Getty Royalty Free and Royalty-Free/CORBIS.

ISBN 0-7398-8973-7

© 2006 Harcourt Achieve Inc.

Printed in the United States of America.
  2 3 4 5 6 7 8   018   10 09 08 07 06

Contents

A HURRICANE STORY

by Ana Menéndez

He hoped for the best but prepared for the worst.

We were standing in the kitchen, watching my mother make tuna sandwiches.

"Tomorrow we'll have to get up early and check the gas pipes," my father said. He turned to me. "Maybe you can help me clean up outside. There will be branches and trash all over."

"I hope we have electricity," my mother said.

"We might not," my father said.

"The TV said to fill the bathtub with water," I said.

"Good idea," my father said. "Why don't you be in charge of that."

I smiled.

My father began to sing in his clear voice.

Yo soy un hombre sincero, de donde crece la palma[1]…

He stopped singing and said suddenly, "The roads might be flooded. We might have to inflate your raft." He winked at me. "You know, it will keep raining for a couple of days," he said. "The thunderstorms come after. Sometimes tornadoes."

"What if the roof leaks?" my mother said.

"We'll have to check it first thing," he said. "Then we'll just take some chewing gum …"

He looked at my mother, who couldn't resist a small smile.

My father turned off the television and as we ate our sandwiches, we talked more about what we would do to prepare. We'd put flashlights in both rooms, for when the power went out. My mother said she would put the milk in the freezer so it would stay fresh and cold no matter what.

We sat and talked and then we were silent, having planned for everything. My mother read a magazine. My father turned a page in his book. I noticed the house was very quiet. Not just inside, but outside. There wasn't the usual sound of cars. And the space between the plywood[2] and the glass was silent. I could no longer hear the branches.

"The storm should be getting close," my father said. We sat and waited. The day was almost over when I put down the book I was reading.

"Tell me again the story of the hurricane," I said. "Tell me about the flying coconuts."

My father looked up and smiled.

"Let's go check the plywood again and I'll tell you how we got the water out of my father's car."

My father looked at my mother.

"You two go," she said.

I stepped outside and was momentarily blinded by the brightness. I blinked and waited for my father to join me. A few thin white clouds floated west in a deepening blue sky. I looked again. A few thin white clouds floated west. The trees swayed back and forth, gently, as if hypnotized. The air smelled of grass and dirt and fresh cuttings. I looked up and down the

A Hurricane Story

street and saw that ours was the only house boarded up. Mr. Hanson's house had tape on the windows. And the Cardelli family had lowered their awnings over their porch and windows. But my father was the only one who had gone through all the trouble with the plywood. I couldn't bear to turn back and look at it now.

My father looked up at the sky, but didn't say anything for a while. We both stood there outside the front door, looking out.

"Well," my father said. "This is how they are sometimes. They seem to come out of nowhere."

I looked up at him. I noticed for the first time the lines around his eyes, how his left one seemed to

A Hurricane Story

droop into a crevice. Above my father, the branches of the live oak played against each other and then were stilled. I looked at my father for a long time like that, his face framed by those branches and the blue sky beyond. At the top of the street, a boy was slowly riding his bicycle in circles. A car horn sounded far away. My father began to whistle.

* * *

I am quiet, thinking.

"So?" he says. "What happened?"

"What do you mean?"

"What happened that night?"

"Isn't it obvious?" I say.

"It never hit?"

"Struck farther up the coast," I say. I consider it for a moment and then add, "I lay in bed that night and couldn't sleep."

He is quiet.

"Do you suppose," he says after a moment, "that your father's stories were true?"

I lay in bed that night as a girl, thinking of big sky and coconuts raining down. I saw our house, hugging itself as if it were afraid of what the wind might bring. I heard my parents whispering a long time into the night. And then they were quiet and the wind outside was quiet. I was embarrassed for our house, standing there like that in the dark. I wanted to hug my father, tell him we were so lucky after all.

---

1 *Yo soy un hombre sincero, de donde crece la palma*: I am a sincere man, from where the palms grow.
2 plywood: thin wood placed over windows to protect them from a storm

The Life and Art of Frida Kahlo

by Jana Martin

Only after her death did she get the recognition she deserved.

Frida Kahlo, born in 1907, is now considered the greatest Mexican painter of the twentieth century and is one of the most well-known women artists in the world. But during her lifetime, she did not achieve the recognition she deserved.

Kahlo's paintings were entirely original. They looked like no other paintings done during her day or at any point in the twentieth century. She painted self-portraits that were primitive, yet elegant. Her work combined aspects of surrealism—a kind of art that portrays the landscape of the mind and dreams—with imagery from Mexican culture and folklore. The surrealist poet Andre Breton called her paintings "a ribbon around a bomb," as they were both delightful to look at and deeply disturbing. Kahlo painted with masterful brushwork and an expert sense of color. She was brilliant at combining delicate details and rich, vivid colors with violent themes.

Kahlo was once asked why she painted so many self-portraits. In fact, she hardly painted anything else besides self-portraits. She responded, "Because I am the subject that I know best." With her tremendous intelligence and spirit in the face of great physical pain and tragedy, she would have been a fascinating subject for any artist. In many of her paintings, you can find elements from her life story and difficult past; images of injuries, bones, and blood fill her work.

Kahlo was born in 1907 to a Hungarian Jewish father and a Mexican Native American mother. Her father was a portrait photographer; her mother was uneducated. They lived in Coyoacan, Mexico. Though her father was close to her, her mother kept her distance, as she never recovered from the death of her son. Kahlo was stricken with polio at the age of six, and the disease left her right leg twisted and shortened. It also eventually twisted her hipbone and spine. But polio was only the first of many physical tragedies she would endure.

As a child, Kahlo got into a lot of mischief. In high school, she was part of a group of students, mostly boys, who were always pulling pranks. In 1925, when she was 18, her life of freedom ground to a halt. She was riding the bus one day when a trolley slammed into it. The accident took many lives and left Kahlo's body pierced through by a railing. Her injuries included broken ribs, a broken hipbone and leg, and a completely crushed right foot.

Healing involved a seemingly endless hospital stay and a long series of difficult operations. Kahlo had to wear a full-body cast that kept her from moving. She was then virtually imprisoned in a box-like apparatus that kept her bones in their correct positions. When she was freed of that but still confined to bed, she began to paint. From the beginning, she was interested in self-portraits.

Some critics have pointed out that Frida Kahlo didn't set out to be a painter but created art out of boredom, or the need to express herself. In any case, once Kahlo became a painter, she found her passion. She was fiercely devoted to her art. When she had recuperated from the accident, she took up the lively life of a typical young woman in Mexico City in the late 1920s. Despite her physical pain, Kahlo was usually in high spirits. She hid her physical problems as best she could. Kahlo was introduced to a number of Mexican artists and writers. One of them, the artist Diego Rivera, she had met before. Rivera had painted a mural at her high school while she was a student there. When the young, inexperienced Kahlo showed the older, well-established Rivera her paintings, he was deeply impressed, struck by the force and depth of her expression. He encouraged her to keep painting. In 1929, they married.

The small young woman and the large mature man made an unusual couple. Their marriage was marked by fights and creative conflicts. Their lives were anything but routine. They were united by their passion for politics and were extremely active in the issues of their day. At one time they considered themselves sympathetic to communism.[1] (Kahlo's circle of friends included the former Russian leader Leon Trotsky.) Kahlo even changed her "official" birth date to 1910 to match the date of Mexico's independence. But most of all, Rivera and Kahlo shared a powerful need to make art.

In some ways, Diego Rivera was extremely supportive of his wife. It was he who suggested that Kahlo dress in her beloved traditional Mexican outfits. But in other ways, Rivera overwhelmed Kahlo with his own artistic ego and drive. Rivera was at the height of his career when Kahlo was fighting for recognition. Rivera's murals were sweeping pictures of Mexican history and socialist ideals, while Kahlo's

The Life and Art of Frida Kahlo

paintings—all self-portraits—dealt with the very private scars and tragedies in her own life. In their personalities they were contrasting as well. Rivera was very outgoing, dramatic, and forceful, while Kahlo, though always lively, was also extremely private. Of course, she often was exhausted, literally, by the physical pain she continued to endure. In 1932, when Rivera was invited to work at the Detroit Institute of the Arts, Kahlo, who was pregnant, accompanied him. But while there, she lost the baby. It was another tragedy for which she found little comfort in those around her.

Kahlo noted to her friends that being near Rivera made her feel even smaller than she actually was, and she expressed that feeling in her work. In one painting, she depicts herself as a small figure in a red cloak next to a towering, portly Rivera. Rivera looks as if he's standing over his wife like a father, or, some critics have noted, like a judge. In another painting—done shortly after she divorced Rivera in 1939—Kahlo gave up her image as a long-haired wife in a Mexican dress. In this painting she shows herself as a woman with cropped hair, holding an open pair of scissors in one hand, a lock of her own hair in the other, and wearing a man's suit. The painting, entitled *Self-Portrait with Cropped Hair*, is now in the permanent collection at New York City's Museum of Modern Art. Critics have noted that Kahlo explores both male and female roles in this picture. She intentionally painted herself seated and looking frankly at the viewer in a bold way. Kahlo was a strong supporter of women's rights and throughout her career worked to overturn traditional ideas about women's roles and behaviors.

Despite their conflicts, Kahlo and Rivera soon remarried. They would remain together until Kahlo's death. In 1941, they moved into Kahlo's childhood home, Casa Azul (The Blue House), and enjoyed the company of many great artists and intellectuals. Although Kahlo did not become fully recognized as an artist until after her death, those who knew her admired the woman and the work. She had an exhibition in New York in 1938, in Paris in 1939, and in Mexico City in 1953. Her supporters included Nelson Rockefeller, an avid sponsor of modern art. She had dinner with Pablo Picasso. Kahlo and Rivera were friends with such artists as Marcel Duchamp and Yves Tanguy, leading French surrealists of the day. Many of these successful, gifted people saw Kahlo as a force to be reckoned with.

Among Kahlo's best-known paintings are *The Broken Column*, *Self-Portrait with Monkey*, and *The Wounded Stag*. The first of these focuses on the spine injury Kahlo sustained in the bus crash. In *Self-Portrait with Monkey*, Kahlo paints herself with a monkey on her shoulder. She's wearing a primitive-looking necklace of bones and shells, her long hair swept up; the monkey looks contented, its arm on her shoulder, a glimmer of mischief in its eyes. But eight years later, another self-portrait with an animal shows a far darker vision. *Wounded Stag* depicts a stag, or deer, shot with many arrows, all of which are drawing blood; in place of its head Frida has substituted her own. The stag looks as if it is running through a bleak forest. The trees have an eerie look, without leaves or life.

By 1953, when Kahlo had her triumphant one-woman show in Mexico City, the artist was in poor health from the injuries and physical problems she'd suffered throughout her life. Doctors told her she needed another series of operations, and the pain she was then enduring left her in a deep depression. At the opening of her show, she arrived on a stretcher, by ambulance, and was arranged on a four-post bed. Guests greeted her with much praise and applause, and it was a high moment in the artist's life. But soon afterwards, she had another setback when her right leg, which had become badly infected, had to be removed.

Kahlo's last year was a tragic one. She dosed herself with more medicines than her doctors allowed. This took its toll on her emotional balance, as well as on her already decreasing physical strength. On July 13, 1954, she died. Among her closest friends and family, many thought she had been so depressed that she took her own life. She received a funeral in Mexico City that was fit for a hero.

Some twenty years after her death, Kahlo began to gain international recognition. She had not been completely respected by the traditional art world—perhaps, some have argued, because she was a woman whose main subject was herself, and perhaps also because she was Latin American. But over the years, opinions and ideas in the art world regarding Kahlo's work changed. Scholars began writing her biography, art critics were exploring the many images and issues in her work, and museums were trying to collect as many of her paintings as they could. Recently, a Kahlo painting sold for $3.2 million—the largest sum ever paid for a Latin American work of art. The actress Salma Hayek starred in a movie based on Kahlo's life. But the most touching memorial to Kahlo is her home, in Mexico City. The Casa Azul has been turned into a museum in Kahlo's name, filled with exhibits of objects and paintings. Some of its rooms look just as they did when she and Rivera lived in them. The brightly-painted kitchen is decorated with Mexican pottery. Among the museum's treasures is a looking-glass in Kahlo's bedroom. It is the mirror from which she painted many of her self-portraits. If visitors stand and gaze into it, they may be able to imagine what it must have been like to see life through her remarkable eyes.

[1] communism: a system of government in which a single political party controls the economy and all goods are equally shared by the people

Mother Hale's Babies

by Irene Virag

With strong love, she has made a big difference.

A freezing wind whips past the young man in Army fatigues as he walks down West 123rd Street. The trash stirs in the gutters, and the broken windows patched with cardboard and lined with newspapers rattle in their cracked frames. The man shoves his hands into his pockets and walks a little faster, unaware of the buildings that have been gutted by fire and deserted by landlords. At the corner, a tall woman in jeans and a matted fake-fur jacket hands him a roll of money. He gives her a packet and says something, but the words are lost in the wind.

The woman nods and walks away. She stops in the middle of the sidewalk and looks over her shoulder before she starts up the stairs that lead into an abandoned building. The long dark hallway is open to the street, where drug buys are everyday business.

One block to the south, in the midst of these rundown Harlem streets where people guard their children against rats, a five-story house stands out against the burnt-out, boarded up buildings that hide heroin[1] addicts and the homeless. There are metal grates on the windows, and the iron gate in front of the house is securely latched. In December, a string

Mother Hale's Babies

of Christmas lights decorates the fire escape, and in the spring, two small trees in the front courtyard tender their green buds as a sign that even in this neighborhood, where everything seems old and worn-out, life can start anew.

Inside this house, a 79-year-old great-grandmother in a green and red apron provides the kind of special support that restores life itself. She offers this support to the female drug addicts who haunt these streets and to the babies they bear.

Mother Hale's Babies

Her name is Clara Hale, but everyone calls her mother—the daughter and son she bore, the boy she adopted years ago, the 40 foster children she raised, the drug-addicted women she has helped, and the 500 babies she has held in her arms while they cried and trembled their way through withdrawal.[2] Even the old men on the corner and the women who wait at the bus stop know her as Mother Hale.

The babies she cradles in her house enter this world with drugs in their blood. They are born addicted to the heroin and cocaine[3] their mothers buy on West 123rd Street.

The babies are brought to Hale House by city social workers and local ministers and priests, by nurses and doctors and the drug counselors who treat addicts about to become mothers. Sometimes, they are carried in by their desperate mothers, who learn about Clara Hale from drug dealers or fellow addicts. When they move into Clara Hale's third-floor bedroom, these newborns begin the battle to overcome their inherited habit. They must go cold turkey. Mother Hale does not allow drugs, even drugs that would lessen the pain of withdrawal, in her home.

In an old rocking chair, Clara Hale soothes her hurting babies. "They cry, how they cry," she says. "They're crying for something they don't understand, for drugs. Sometimes I cry with them, but mostly I sing—church hymns, little snatches of songs from my childhood. I talk to them, too. I tell them I love them. I tell them God loves them. And, always, I tell them their mothers love them."

Every morning she wakes in time to give a 6 a.m. bottle to each of the three babies who share her bedroom. It is the first of many trips up and down the three flights of stairs for the thin, gray-haired woman who loves her babies as if she gave birth to them. She changes their diapers, she cleans the vomit they spit up, and she holds them close when withdrawal makes them shaky and impossible to comfort. She feeds them lunch and dinner and she naps when they nap. Every addicted baby who comes to Hale House lives in "mommy's room" for the first four to six months.

Then they move to the lower floors, where flowers and children's finger paintings brighten the walls and the ex-addicts who have yet to reach their second birthdays are watched over by trained child-care workers until their mothers can take them home. When they are three or four, some of them come back to Hale House for its day-care program.

But it is the work that takes place in Mother Hale's royal blue bedroom that makes her house unique. "For a while, all they do is frown and squirm and scratch and cry," she says in a voice that is soft from all the years of whispering to infants. "I rock them and wait. I know they're trying, so I wait, because I know that one day they'll smile at me."

As she talks, Clara Hale rocks a baby named Shannon Baker in her arms. She kisses the three-month-old, who inherited her mother's wide dark eyes and addiction to heroin and cocaine, a habit that cost Mary Baker $300 a day and three older children who have been placed in foster homes.

"I cried when I saw Mama Hale," the 39-year-old mother recalled. "I asked her to take my baby and forgive me. I felt so guilty."

Clara Hale tells the mothers of her babies not to cry. She does not deal in guilt. "You made a mistake," she tells women like Mary Baker. "You are a drug addict. You can change. Mistakes can be corrected."

One of Clara Hale's rules is that they try. Like all mothers who leave their children in the house, Mary Baker entered a rehabilitation clinic[4] to be placed on a methadone[5] maintenance program.

Now the mother and child are together in Clara Hale's room, where clean diapers are stacked in a corner and two cribs are positioned close to her bed and one wall is filled with photographs of her 40 foster children. It is another rule that mothers must visit their babies at least once a week. "They must get to know each other and to love each other," Clara Hale says. "I don't run an adoption agency. Children belong with their mothers. They all go home when the mothers are ready for them." In 16 years, only a dozen of the 500 drug-addicted babies who have come to Hale House have been put up for adoption.

As Clara Hale places Shannon into her mother's arms, she rubs her lined cheek across the baby's soft skin. "I love you, sweet little baby girl. I will help you. Ssshhh. I love all the sweet little babies in the world."

She whispers these words to the baby as if she is revealing a well-kept secret. But it is a simple truth that is legend on these mean streets—the reason she has received awards from the local police and community centers, from groups of senior citizens and narcotics[6] officers, from the NAACP and the Wonder Woman Foundation. It is the reason she gets more than $175,000 a year from New York City's Special Services for Children and an annual donation of $20,000 from Yoko Ono, which was started by John Lennon before his death. It is the reason she is called the "leading authority on drug-addicted infants" by officials in the New York State Division of Substance Abuse. She is an authority through years of painful observation.

"All I know about drugs is that they destroy," she says. "What I know is about babies. That's how this whole thing started."

It started in the 1940s, when a young widow whose husband had died of cancer took in other women's children so she could support three of her own. Many of the mothers paid Clara Hale to care for the children while they went off to work as live-in maids. After 20 years as the neighborhood nanny and a foster parent who received $2 a week per child from the city, Clara Hale, at 63, took in her first drug-poisoned baby.

The baby was a three-month-old girl, whom Mother Hale remembers only as a "wide-eyed beauty." Clara Hale was ready to quit mothering, proud of the fact that none of her charges had ever been arrested, that her three children and 40 foster children had all gone to college. Then her daughter, Lorraine, saw a heroin addict sleeping in a gutter with a baby in her arms. She roused the woman and gave her Clara Hale's address.

"I told her, 'Here is where you can get help,'" recalled Doctor Lorraine Hale, who is the director of

Hale House. "My mother has always been committed to the belief that there is goodness in every person. She feels it is her responsibility to respect and honor everyone. I knew she wouldn't turn that baby away."

Within a month, Clara Hale had 22 addicted babies in her five-room apartment on West 146th St. "Before I knew it," Clara Hale says, "every pregnant addict in Harlem knew about the crazy lady who would give her baby a home."

Within five years, she had the five-story house where she sings "Amazing Grace" to Shannon Baker on a windy winter afternoon. The baby with the wide dark eyes listens as if she understands every word of Mother Hale's favorite hymn.

Clara Hale kisses Shannon's cheek and rubs her neck and tells Mary Baker, "That's a sweet baby you have there, girl. Be good to her." And the woman who offers the kind of special support that can restore life itself closes the door and lies down for a nap.

In the corner of the room, Mary Baker sits in the rocker with her baby in her arms. Quietly, she sings: "Amazing Grace, how sweet the sound that saved a wretch like me. I once was lost, but now I'm found, was blind but now I see."

[1] heroin: a strongly addictive (habit-forming) drug
[2] withdrawal: the act of stopping the use of a drug
[3] cocaine: a drug of abuse
[4] rehabilitation clinic: a place for the medical treatment of addicts
[5] methadone: a hard-drug substitute used to aid addicts in breaking their addition to heroin
[6] narcotics: concerned with drugs

DON'T PANIC!

by Esteban Gonzales

**You feel dizzy. You can't breathe. Don't worry—
it's only a panic attack.**

Picture this: You're walking through the mall, and
all of a sudden you feel short of breath. You notice
your heart is racing, and you're sweating. You begin
to feel scared and wonder what is happening. You
may ask yourself, "What's wrong with me?"

Each year, many people visit doctors, trying to figure out what their problem is. They are searching for
reasons for these attacks of nervousness, sweaty
palms, a queasy stomach, or lightheadedness.

The first time you experience a panic attack, you
may go to a doctor, only to be told there's nothing physically wrong. So you try to reason with yourself: "If
nothing is wrong with me, then I'll just try to stay calm
and this miserable feeling will go away." But it seems
the harder you try, the more frequently it returns.

Symptoms of a panic attack include:
- racing heartbeat
- difficulty breathing, feeling as though you "can't get
  enough air"
- terror that is almost paralyzing
- dizziness or upset stomach
- trembling, sweating, shaking
- choking or chest pains
- hot flashes or sudden chills
- tingling in fingers or toes ("pins and needles")
- fear that you're going to go crazy or are about to die

A lack of chemical balance in your body can cause you to feel anxious. You are not mentally ill, but if the fear that you have is not based on a physical illness and compels you to avoid normal, everyday things that most people deal with easily, you may have a phobia. Phobias can go hand in hand with anxiety and panic attacks.

A panic attack is not dangerous, but it can be terrifying, largely because it feels "crazy" and "out of control." Panic disorder can lead to other complications such as depression and medical problems. It can affect your speech in a mild way or make you feel totally unable to face the outside world.

Don't Panic!   **21**

Experts are not sure what causes panic disorders. For some people, these reactions may be part of their natural makeup. Some sufferers report that a family member has or had a panic disorder or another type of emotional disorder, such as depression. Studies with twins have suggested the possibility that panic disorders might be inherited. Of course, stressful life events, such as a recent loss, can trigger panic disorders.

In fact, the phobias that people with panic disorder develop do not come from fears of actual objects or events, but rather from the fear of having another attack. In these cases, people will avoid certain objects or situations because they fear that these things will trigger another attack. For instance, their "fear of flying" is not that the plane will crash but that they will have a panic attack in a place where they can't get to help. Others will avoid climbing a ladder or riding in an elevator because they're afraid that these situations might trigger the physical signs of a panic attack. Physical and mental causes of panic disorder work together. Although attacks may initially come out of the blue, eventually the sufferer may help bring them on by responding to physical signs of an attack.

Many people experience occasional panic attacks. If you have had one or two such attacks, there probably isn't any reason to worry. The key symptom of panic disorder is the persistent fear of having future panic attacks. If you suffer from repeated (four or more) panic attacks, and especially if you have had a panic attack and are in fear of having another, these are signs that you should consider finding a mental health professional who specializes in panic or anxiety disorders. A doctor can tell you whether your fear exceeds a normal response to a situation.

Without treatment, panic disorders can have very serious consequences. The immediate danger with a panic disorder is that it can often lead to a phobia, a powerful fear that is not based on reality. That's because once you've suffered a panic attack, you may start to avoid situations like the one you were in when the attack occurred.

Many people with panic disorders avoid places and experiences that they associate with their panic attacks. For example, you might have an attack while driving and then keep away from the wheel until you develop an actual phobia towards cars. In worst-case situations, people with panic disorder develop agoraphobia—fear of open or public places—because they believe that by staying inside, they can escape from all situations that might provoke an attack. The fear of an attack is so strong that these people prefer to spend their lives locked inside their homes rather than go to work or enjoy a pleasant excursion.

Even if you don't develop these extreme phobias, your quality of life can be severely damaged by untreated panic disorder. A recent study showed that people who suffer from panic disorder spend more time in hospital emergency rooms and less time on hobbies, sports, and other satisfying activities. They tend to rely upon others for help with money issues and report feeling emotionally and physically less healthy than non-sufferers.

Some Common and Unusual Phobias

acousticophobia—fear of noise
acrophobia—fear of heights
ancraophobia—fear of wind
arachibutyrophobia—fear of peanut butter
  sticking to the roof of the mouth
arachnophobia—fear of spiders
belonephobia—fear of pins and needles
catoptrophobia—fear of mirrors
claustrophobia—fear of enclosed spaces
cometophobia—fear of comets
coulrophobia—fear of clowns
eisoptrophobia—fear of mirrors
gephyrophobia—fear of crossing a bridge
herpetophobia—fear of reptiles
hypnophobia—fear of sleep
scotophobia—fear of the dark
thanatophobia—fear of death
toxiphobia, toxicophobia—fear of being poisoned
triskaidekaphobia—fear of the number 13
xenophobia—fear or hatred of foreigners
  and strange things
zoophobia—fear of animals

Panic disorders can also have financial effects. For example, a recent study cited the case of a woman who gave up a $40,000 a year job that required travel for one close to home that only paid $14,000 a year. Other sufferers have reported losing their jobs and having to rely on family members. In many cases, the person loses a sense of vitality and well-being.

The good news is that anxiety and panic attacks can usually be treated in more than one way. Most specialists agree that a combination of treatments is the best way to deal with panic disorder. Medicines might also be appropriate in some cases. These medicines can help people to calm down, but they seldom cure the problem.

If you exhibit any of the symptoms mentioned earlier, first go to your regular doctor to rule out any medical conditions that may be causing these problems. If you are in good health, the doctor should realize that you may be suffering from anxiety and panic attacks and refer you to a psychologist[1] for some talk therapy.

Here are some things a psychologist may have you try after he or she examines you and decides that you are suffering from panic attacks:

1. **Use Your Imagination**:

    Picture yourself with a relaxed look on your face at work and at home.

    Picture yourself refusing requests that will cause you to overwork.

    See yourself being able to participate in hobbies that you have avoided out of fear.

2. **Be Positive**:

    Tell yourself that you feel perfectly normal and that you can do any activity that you want.

    Tell yourself that you are worthy of the love of others even when you don't think that you are.

When you wake up in the morning, look at yourself in the mirror and repeat positive statements to yourself. You can find many books in the bookstore

Don't Panic!

or library on positive thinking. Make them part of your everyday routine.

3. **Rethink Your Thinking:**

   If you suffer from panic attacks, it's important to identify possible triggers, or causes, for the frightening feelings. The trigger in an individual case could be something like a thought, a situation, or something as slight as a change in heartbeat. Once a person understands that the panic attack is separate and independent of the trigger, that trigger begins to lose some of its power to cause an attack.

4. **Relaxation Exercises:**

   Teach yourself how to breathe correctly. Most of us breathe from our upper chest area instead of our lower chest area. Practice deep breathing. Studies have found that it is impossible to have a panic attack when you are inhaling and exhaling deeply and properly.

Relax your mind and body, and get some exercise. A healthy person can survive panic attacks. Exercising can be the best treatment. You will have a new and exciting lifestyle if you are experiencing high levels of health. You will find it easier to exercise and eat right if you picture yourself doing positive things.

The bottom line is that anxiety and panic attacks are 100% treatable. Don't suffer more than you have to. Take charge and get yourself on the track to a better quality of life. It may take some work, but it will be worth it.

[1] psychologist: a doctor who studies and treats problems of the mind and behavior.

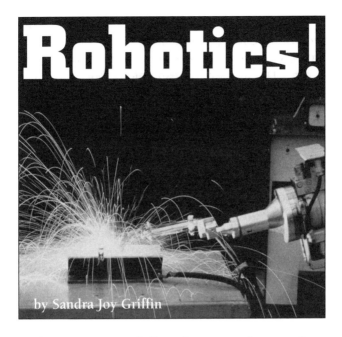

Robotics!

by Sandra Joy Griffin

Robots are a great help to humans—but are they a threat to take over the world?

What do you see when you picture a robot? Perhaps you see a kind of two-legged, stiff-walking machine-creature with antennae, glowing coils, and blinking dials. That's the way many science fiction writers and artists have pictured robots in the past. But do you know what a robot actually is? A robot is a machine that imitates the actions or appearance of a human or an animal and can work on its own after it is programmed by humans. Every robot must have a body, be controlled by a human programmer, and perform some action—it must do something!

Based on these three essential elements, which of the following are robots: a camera? a lamp? a wristwatch? a car? a CD player? A camera, a lamp, a wristwatch, and a CD player are probably not robots. However, some objects that don't seem to be robotic can be considered robots, depending on the task. For example, a car is not a robot, but when you are using the automatic "cruise control" feature, the car becomes a kind of robot. Robots can range from simple machines to highly complex, computer-controlled devices.

Robots are designed to perform many different kinds of work. In order to be fully functional, the machine must have a robotic arm. A robotic arm usually has the following five parts:

1. Controller—the "brain" of the computer that programs the machine
2. Arm—the part that positions the "hand" and sensors
3. Drive—the engine, which is powered by air, water pressure, or electricity
4. "Hand"—the part connected to the arm, which performs the task
5. Sensor—the part that sends information in the form of electric signals back to the controller (For example, the sensor may be able to detect radiation.)

Many robotic arms have shoulders, elbows, wrists, and even fingers. These help the robot to do things in the place of a human. A mechanical arm that can move in at least six ways has six "degrees of freedom." Each degree is a direction in which a joint can move. A robot arm must be able to move in a circular way at its base; move up and down at its base; bend its elbow; move its wrist up and down; move its wrist left and right; and rotate its wrist.

The History of Robots

The word *robot* comes from the Czech word *robota*, meaning hard, boring work or slave-like labor. It was first used to describe fictional workers in a 1923 play by the Czech author Karel Capek. The name of the play was *Rossum's Universal Robots* (*RUR*). In the play, a scientist invents robots that can perform simple tasks in order to help people. However, once the robots are used to fight wars, they turn on their human owners and take over the world. Since 1923, robots have been featured in the movies and on television programs. They have played all kinds of roles, from super-human heroes to destructive villains. It seems that we humans are not absolutely comfortable with these electronic helpers.

Robots Work!

Robots can do boring or dangerous jobs that people don't want to do. Almost all robots work in factories, mostly car factories, assembling parts. Another job done by robots is the arrangement of chocolates in their boxes. A robotic arm that is guided by a computer locates the piece of chocolate on a moving conveyor belt. Then it gently lifts the chocolate and places it in a box that is moving along on another conveyor belt. Anyone can do this job. But can you imagine doing it 20,000 times a day, every day, for the rest of your life?

Robots can defuse bombs to prevent them from exploding. Guided by a video camera, a robot can place objects in bomb boxes or defuse the bomb directly. The robot's movements can be controlled from a distance by a computer while the humans remain in a safe location.

Robots can also do medical procedures. They can perform certain types of surgery, even delicate eye surgery. This lets surgeons undertake procedures that would be very difficult for human hands.

Robots can also be used as body parts. These are different from a prosthesis, or artificial body part, which is not able to perform tasks. These new body parts can be programmed to imitate human motion and actions.

Robots can even do home chores! Several companies have recently developed a robotic vacuum cleaner that you may have seen advertised. It has a tiny computer chip "brain" and sonar "eyes." It can turn and get in and out of corners. First, the robotic vacuum makes a trip around the edge of the room, and then it continues to cross the room in a random pattern until the entire space is vacuumed. You can program it to do your chores and then do something fun instead. You might simultaneously clean a room and watch a video.

When it comes to having fun, how would you like a pet robot? You can have a robot puppy that can hear and see; it even has a sense of balance and touch. Special motors allow it to roll over, play dead, and chase a ball. It must be trained by its owner, and it can be programmed to imitate emotions like happiness or to respond to commands. You needn't restrain your robotic dog from barking at the mail carrier or chewing up the rug. Best of all, it doesn't shed and you don't have to take it out for a walk!

Robots can also play thinking games. By programming large amounts of information into a computer, people can make robots play games based on complicated rules. It can calculate a complex series of moves. The robot is a form of Artificial Intelligence (AI) that can learn to consider 400 million chess moves per second. IBM's "Deep Blue" robot beat chess champion Garry Kasparov in 1997.

Who knows? Perhaps one day we can combine all of the advances in technology for robotics—medical, artificial intelligence, motion, engineering, and mechanics—so that we can play action games with a robot!

The Future of Robots

Scientists are doing research to develop a new class of robots that will be able to work in places that are not safe for humans. These bio-robots will be programmed for strength and intelligence and built with new state-of-the-art materials. Such a robot might look like an insect and have the power of a large machine.

Code of Conduct

Since a robot can be programmed to do almost anything, it is important for humans to think about some rules of conduct. What is right and wrong for a robot? In 1942, Isaac Asimov, the science fiction writer, proposed a Three-Point Code of Conduct that

Three Laws of Robotics

First Law:

A robot may not injure a human being or through inaction allow a human being to come to harm.

Second Law:

A robot must obey the orders given it by human beings, except where such orders would conflict with the First Law.

Third Law:

A robot must protect its own existence, as long as such protection does not conflict with the First or Second Laws.

has been called the "Three Laws of Robotics."

Robots have been around for nearly a century. They have appeared in stories and movies and have been used in countless toys and games. Today, robots are a reality, and they play a big part in our modern lives. But what will future robots be like? Will they do our shopping, cook our meals, and even take out our garbage? Will they fly our planes or drive our cars? Is it possible that human beings will eventually rely too much on robots? Will robots ever turn against human beings and try to take over the world? Only time will tell …

After the Ball

by Sally Benson

She wanted to put away childish things.

No one could have guessed her age, seeing her drive around town. She drove with her hands resting casually on the wheel. Her lipstick matched her nails and blended with the color of her dress. She was perfect from head to toe. Her manner was perfect too. She spoke in a tired, low-pitched voice, and she looked at the person she was addressing as though he were very far away.

She might have been the spoiled daughter of a millionaire. She might have been anyone romantic and exciting. But her name was Norma Martin, and she'd recently graduated from school. Her hockey stick had been forgotten in the hall closet at home; her schoolbooks had been sold to a child who still believed that being a senior was all that Life could hold. For the Norma Martin summering at Pine Bluffs, school days were gone forever. Pine Bluffs was the Present. It was Life.

The idea of going someplace new, someplace different, had come to her during vacation. She had caught her mother writing to reserve the same cottage at Monroe, Connecticut, that they had rented for the last fourteen years and she realized never again could she stand Monroe. In the first place, there was Annie, with whom she had played every summer for as long as she could remember. Annie was nice, but she was fifteen. When you were only fifteen, you were as good as dead. She knew what it was like to be only fifteen in Monroe. She could see herself as she had been last summer, being a little noisy on the beach to attract the attention of the older crowd. This summer, she knew, she could never bring herself to merely look on. She was sixteen. Pretty soon she would be seventeen, eighteen, nineteen, and then twenty. She would be married at twenty. Twenty would be the end.

After the Ball

So in a panic she begged her mother not to write for their old cottage in Monroe. In desperation she fished a name from her memory—Pine Bluffs. A girl from school had been there once. There, no one would know how old she was. She would have her driver's license, and as far as anyone could tell, she would be as good as eighteen.

Norma didn't paint this picture for her mother. She told her that there was practically no traffic on the roads, which would be good since her mother was so nervous in a car, that there were beautiful drives and free lectures about wild flowers.

Mrs. Martin was won over. "You know, I've been thinking I'd like a change myself," she told her husband.

Mrs. Martin was a little disappointed when she saw the cottage. It was just like the cottage in Monroe. But Norma was delighted. She pronounced the cottage perfect and the swimming marvelous. And she underwent a great change.

She began to fuss over her appearance, spending hours in the tub, hours over her nails, hours getting dressed. It seemed to Mrs. Martin that Norma was always underfoot. It was nice, she thought, that the child was beginning to take an interest in her appearance, but it had been nice, too, in the days when she was up, out of the house, and out of the way. Mrs. Martin didn't understand why Norma spent so much time staring at herself in the mirror anyway; there didn't seem to be much for her to look special for.

Although they had been at Pine Bluffs ten days, Norma knew no one. Every morning, she drove to the village to do the marketing. She was so proud of her driving and there were so few places to drive that Mrs. Martin had agreed to let her go. By the time the marketing was done, it was time for lunch—a salad for Norma and a glass of orange juice. "You've got to eat!" Mrs. Martin cried in desperation over this strict diet.

"First you tell me I'm too fat, and then you tell me I'm too thin," Norma answered.

Then one day Mrs. Martin came back from the beach with good news. "Norma!" she called. "What do you think? I met the nicest woman on the beach, and she has a daughter named Jerry. Anyway, she is having a beach picnic tonight and they want you to come."

For a second there was a brief flicker of excitement in Norma's face. But almost immediately, she assumed her usual blank expression.

"How old is she?"

"I don't know," her mother said. "About your age, I'd say. Fifteen or sixteen."

"Mother!" Norma exclaimed. "A kid! A child!"

"She's no more a child than you are," Mrs. Martin argued. "What's gotten into you?"

"You haven't found out as much about this place as I have," Norma told her. "There are two groups, not counting the babies. There are the kids, fourteen or fifteen, and then there's the older crowd. And if you once go around with the kids, you're absolutely finished with the older crowd. You might as well be dead."

Things went on as they had been, until Norma met Bill James. He had talked to her at the garage where she was having a tire changed, and later that day he had stopped by their cottage.

After the Ball

"So this is your first summer here," he said kindly to Mrs. Martin. "Well, you're going to love it. It's a great crowd. There are the Harrises, the Waites, Dizzy Thomas, the Smith girls . . ." He reeled off names. "It's a close-knit group," he told them. But he looked at Norma and his eyes seemed to say, "Don't worry, I'll get you in."

That night Mrs. Martin wrote her husband. "It's awful here," she wrote. She went on to tell him about Bill James. "I don't know what to do. If I put my foot down and forbid her to see him, Norma will hate me."

To Norma she said, "The people here sound very dull. I should think you'd be bored. Why, they're older people. Some of them are married and some are engaged. That Bill James is twenty-six. Ten years older than you. The idea!"

But Norma, it seemed, was not bored. She was impressed and pleased to have the attention. "There's to be a dance at the community hall this Saturday," she told her mother. "It's the first one."

She went to her closet and took out her three evening dresses, the old one from last winter and two new ones.

"Which one would you wear?" she asked.

"Well, I always loved that blue one on you," Mrs. Martin said. "It's a sweet dress."

"It's too sweet. It makes me look about twelve." She laid it aside.

"Are you going with Bill?"

"Oh, I imagine so," Norma answered confidently. "He hasn't asked yet. Of course, the tickets are twenty dollars apiece, and he hasn't a lot of money."

The day before the dance, Norma came home from the beach white and tearful. She came alone and she began talking before she was in the house. "Oh, Mother! The most terrible thing happened! We were sitting around at Bill's, and Diz got fooling with my bag. She wanted to borrow my lipstick, she said. But I think she was just snooping, because all the girls looked at one another as if they'd put her up to it. She found my driver's license! And read it!"

"Well, what about it?" Mrs. Martin asked. "There's nothing to be ashamed of on your driver's license. You've never been arrested for anything."

"But now they know!" Norma cried. "And they acted so funny!"

"Know what?" Mrs. Martin was puzzled.

"How old I am! They know how old I am!"

"Do you mean to tell me that no one knew how old you are?" Mrs. Martin was shocked.

"Of course not! You don't think for one minute that Bill or any of them would have paid any attention to me for one minute if they'd known I was sixteen, do you? They thought I was about eighteen. I'm through. They'll drop me. You ought to hear how they joke about the kids. You ought to see how they acted. They said, 'You old cradle-snatcher, you,' to Bill. And he didn't like it, let me tell you."

Bill James did not come that day, nor did he come the next. "Well, now you know what he's like," Mrs. Martin said scornfully.

About nine, when the cars began to go by the house and the music at the community hall started, Mrs. Martin pulled down the shades of the front

After the Ball

windows. "Those moths," she said brightly. "I can't stand hearing them beat their wings on the screen."

It was about twelve when there was a knock at the door, and Mrs. Martin heard Bill James's voice. He was feeling great. The party was going like a forest fire, and he had come to take Norma to the dance.

"Hop into your things," he said.

Mrs. Martin waited sickeningly for Norma's answer. "If she is grateful, I'll die," she thought.

Then Norma's voice came to her, cool and fresh. "I couldn't, not possibly. It's late."

"Late!" Bill James laughed. "It's only twelve! We've got three hours! It's the crest of the evening, and I'm on the crest of the wave!"

"No, really," Norma said coldly. "Thanks just the same."

There was silence in the living room. "Well, if you won't come..." Bill James said, no longer sounding confident.

"No. No, thank you," Norma answered. "I don't feel like it, really. Thanks for dropping by."

Mrs. Martin's bedroom door opened suddenly and Norma's head looked in. "Did you hear that?" she asked. "Coming around this time of night! Who does he think he is? What does he think I am?"

She smiled gaily at her mother and added, as an afterthought, "Why, he's over the hill, and I wouldn't be caught dead going to a dance with someone that old!"

GREGORY
Hines
THE IMMACULATE PERFORMER

by Yuri Skujins

He was a film actor, theater star, and the greatest tap dancer of his generation.

On the evening of September 21, 2003, the historic Apollo Theater in New York City's Harlem held a tribute to one of America's most beloved and respected entertainers, Gregory Hines. Stars of Hollywood and Broadway such as Laurence Fishburne, Phylicia Rashad, and Ossie Davis joined many others to celebrate the life and career of this multitalented entertainer. Gregory Hines had died of cancer on August 9, 2003, at the age of 57. Why did all these stars of the stage and screen gather together to honor this man? Perhaps they knew that one of our era's true originals had passed away. For Gregory Hines had been a fiercely talented, ambitious, and generous African-American man who had earned a very special reputation in the exciting world of popular culture.

Gregory Oliver Hines was born on February 14, 1946, in New York City. Recognizing his talent, Gregory's mother and father were eager to make sure that he and his older brother, Maurice Jr., had every opportunity to escape the grinding poverty that surrounded them. They encouraged their sons to study tap dance, and the boys soon began developing their own tap dance routines. Later Gregory said, "I don't remember not dancing. When I realized I was alive and these were my parents, and I could walk and talk, I could dance." The brothers soon formed an act, The Hines Kids. They performed at the Apollo Theater for two weeks in 1952 when Gregory was only six! In 1954, Maurice and Gregory were cast in the Broadway musical *The Girl in Pink Tights*, starring French ballerina Jeanmaire.

It was during this time that young Gregory found a series of mentors who recognized his talent and encouraged him to work hard at his craft. He studied dance with master tap dancer Henry Le Tang and learned from more mature performers and show business veterans such as the Nicholas Brothers, Honi Coles, and Sandman Sims. Performing, rehearsing, and just hanging around the Broadway stages and dance studios exposed young Gregory to many talented and driven people who took a shine to the ambitious young man. Their advice and encouragement was something Gregory Hines never forgot.

As they grew older, The Hines Kids grew into the Hines Brothers. When Gregory was eighteen, he and Maurice were joined by their father, Maurice Sr., and the family troupe became known as Hines, Hines and Dad. They performed constantly, making nightclub[1] appearances across the country. They toured internationally and appeared frequently on *The Tonight Show*. Accessible and fun to watch, tap had become popular in the United States. But Gregory began to get restless. He had tired of the relentless, nonstop touring and wanted to explore careers other than dancing. It was during this time that he met and wed his first wife, Patricia Panella.

In his early 20s, Gregory moved to Venice, California. With its laid-back, late-1960s feeling, Venice was a far cry from the hustle of New York City. Gregory formed a jazz/rock band, but that also failed to satisfy him. Still searching for what might bring him the most satisfaction, he left Southern California and soon had a shocking idea. "I felt I didn't want to be in show business anymore. I felt that I wanted to be a farmer," Gregory laughingly told an interviewer years later. Invited to work on a farm in upstate New York, he quickly learned a lesson. Beginning before dawn, "I was milking cows and shoveling terrible stuff and working all day. By the end of the day all I wanted was my tap shoes. I thought, 'What am I doing? I better get back where I belong—on the stage where we work at night and can sleep late!'"

However, all these changes came with a price. His brother Maurice was less influenced by 1960s counterculture[2] and music and had little interest in developing a rock band. So, in 1973, the family act was dissolved, which angered Maurice. This, in turn, caused Gregory much pain. But he stuck to what he felt was right. He knew he had to continue searching to find his place in the world. "I was going through a lot of changes....I was finding myself," said Gregory. The brothers did not speak for years.

Gregory returned to New York City in 1978, partly to be near his daughter, Daria, who was living with his now ex-wife Pamela. He also made up with his brother, who told him to audition for the Broadway-bound musical, *The Last Minstrel Show*. Gregory got the part, but the show opened and closed in Philadelphia, Pennsylvania. Most importantly, however, Gregory was back in the mix! Gregory Hines was once again a major player on the Broadway scene.

Soon, the brothers were reunited onstage in the Broadway musical *Eubie*, a tribute to jazz composer Eubie Blake. Gregory got great reviews. He was praised for his singing of "Low Down Blues" and his tat-tat-tat tapping during the number "Hot Feet." For the first time he was nominated for a Tony award, Broadway's highest honor. Now, Gregory Hines was a hit on Broadway. He earned Tony nominations for his performances in *Comin' Uptown* and *Sophisticated Ladies*. In 1992, he finally won a Tony for best actor in a musical, playing jazz legend "Jelly Roll" Morton in *Jelly's Last Jam*.

Gregory also began to gain the attention of Hollywood casting directors and producers. He landed his first film role in the 1981 Mel Brooks comedy *History of the World Part I*, in which he played a Roman slave. Later that year, he made a convincing medical examiner in the horror film *Wolfen*. In 1984, he was cast as a leading actor in *The Cotton Club*, a big-budget Hollywood feature with

Richard Gere, Diane Lane, and Nicholas Cage. He and Maurice were cast as brothers in the film, which was based on The Cotton Club, an actual Harlem nightclub popular in the 1930s. The Cotton Club was where many African-American entertainers performed for wealthy, whites-only audiences. The film's director, Francis Ford Coppola, encouraged the brothers to improvise, so they based one scene on their real-life reunion in *Eubie*. Later, Gregory admitted that the tears they shared in that mesmerizing scene were real.

In 1985 Gregory starred in *White Nights*, which features one of the best examples of his artistic dance style on film. In this Cold-War-era thriller, Gregory is paired with Mikhail Barishnikov. Barishnikov is considered by many experts to be the greatest classical ballet dancer of the late twentieth century, and this pairing was an inspired bit of casting. There are several dance numbers in the film that show the dazzling talents of these artists. For example, during one practice session the two dancers compete with one another. Mikhail performs a series of difficult and precise classical dance moves, and Gregory responds with equally exciting movements that display his tap/jazz techniques. These exchanges grow more and more intense and finally result in a "dance-off" between the two pride-filled artists. During the dance number, a mutual respect emerges between the dancers. Aside from the great dancing, the movie *White Nights* also deals with a number of important issues, such as classical art versus popular art and the relations between black and white people.

It was during the run of *Jelly's Last Jam* that Gregory first got to work on stage with the young dancer and choreographer, Savion Glover. Savion played the role of the young "Jelly" in the Broadway show. They had first worked together on the 1988 film *Tap*. Remembering the support that he had received from his own mentors, Gregory took Savion under his wing and offered the young artist support and advice. In fact, Gregory wrote the foreword[3] to Savion's book *Savion: My Life in Tap*.

Gregory continued to find success in Hollywood with a string of feature films, including the cop-buddy comedy *Running Scared* and the romantic drama *Waiting to Exhale*. He directed his first film in 1994, an independent feature called *Bleeding Heart*. His work in television was equally exciting. He earned Emmy nominations for his performance in *Motown Returns to the Apollo* (1985) and won a Daytime Emmy for voice performance as "Big Bill" in Bill Cosby's cartoon series *Little Bill* (1999).

In his last few years, Gregory stayed as busy and successful as ever. In 1997, he had a network television comedy, *The Gregory Hines Show*, playing a recently divorced dad trying to re-enter the dating world. In the 1999–2000 television season, he had a role on several episodes of the hit comedy series *Will and Grace*. He was again nominated for an Emmy in 2001 for his lead performance in the cable miniseries *Bojangles*. That year, Gregory won an NAACP[4] Image Award for this work; he had won this award previously for his role in *Running Scared*.

The entertainment world mourned the passing of Gregory Hines in the late summer of 2003. Broadway director George C. Wolfe, the director of *Jelly's Last Jam*, said, "He was the last of a kind of immaculate performer—a singer, dancer, actor, and personality. He knew how to command." That statement echoes what many in the world of arts and entertainment felt for a long time: that Gregory Hines was an American original who gave us so very much.

[1] nightclub: a place that serves food and drink and provides entertainment
[2] counterculture: a part of society that has different values from the mainstream
[3] foreword: a brief introduction to a book written by someone other than the author
[4] NAACP: The National Association for the Advancement of Colored People

Luck

by Mark Twain

Sometimes it is better to be lucky than smart.

It was at a dinner in London in honor of one of the two or three highly distinguished English military names of this generation. For reasons which will presently appear, I will not use his real name and titles and call him General Lord Arthur Scoresby, etc., etc., etc. What a fascination there is in a famous name! There sat the man, in living flesh, whom I had heard of so many thousands of times since that day, thirty years before, when his name suddenly soared to the heights from a Russian battlefield, to remain forever celebrated. It was food and drink to me to look, and look, and look at that god-like figure; scanning, searching, noting: the quietness, the reserve, the noble gravity of his appearance; the simple honesty that expressed itself all over him; the sweet unconsciousness of his greatness—unconsciousness of the deep, loving, sincere worship rising out of the breasts of those people and flowing toward him.

The minister at my left was an old acquaintance of mine—a minister now, but he had spent the first half of his life in the camp and field and as a teacher in the military school at Woolwich. Just at the moment I have been talking about, a veiled and strange light sparkled in his eyes, and he leaned down and muttered quietly to me—indicating the hero of the dinner with a gesture: "Privately—he's an absolute fool."

This judgment was a great surprise to me. My astonishment could not have been greater. Two things I was well aware of: that my friend, the Reverend, was a completely truthful man and that his judgment of men was good. Therefore, I knew beyond doubt or question that the world was mistaken about this hero: he *was* a fool. So I meant to find out, at a convenient moment, how the Reverend, all alone, had discovered the secret.

Some days later the opportunity came, and this is what the Reverend told me:

About forty years ago I was a teacher in the military academy at Woolwich. I was present in one of the sections when young Scoresby underwent his first examination. My heart was touched with pity, for the rest of the class answered up brightly and handsomely, while he—why, dear me, he didn't know anything. He was evidently good and sweet and lovable and sincere; and so it was exceedingly painful to see him stand there as quiet as a stone and deliver himself of answers which were truly miraculous for stupidity and ignorance. All the pity in me was roused in his behalf. I said to myself, when he comes to be examined again he will fail, of course; so it will

be simply a harmless act of charity to ease his fall as much as I can. I took him aside and found that he knew a little ancient history; and as he didn't know anything else, I went to work and drilled him like a galley-slave on a certain line of common questions which I knew would be used. If you'll believe me, he went through with flying colors on examination day! He made it because I stored his memory with facts. And he got compliments too, while others, who knew a thousand times more than he, got plucked. By some strange lucky accident—an accident not likely to happen twice in a century—he was asked no question outside the limits of his narrow drill.

It was astounding. Well, all through his course I stood by him, with something of the feeling which a mother has for a crippled child; and he always saved himself, just by miracle apparently.

Now, of course, the thing that would expose him and kill him at last was mathematics. I resolved to make his death as easy as I could; so I drilled him and drilled him over and over again, just on the line of questions which the examiners would be most likely to use, and then launched him on his fate. Well, sir, try to think of the result; to my dismay, he took the first prize! And he got showered with compliments.

Sleep? There was no more sleep for me for a week. My conscience tortured me day and night. What I had done I had done purely through charity, and only to ease the poor youth's fall. I never had dreamed of any such foolish results as the thing that had happened. I felt guilty and miserable. Here was a wooden-head whom I had put in the way of glittering promotions and heavy responsibilities, and but one thing could happen: he and his responsibilities would all go to ruin together at the first opportunity.

A war had just broken out. Of course there had to be a war, I say to myself. We could have peace and give this donkey a chance to die before he is found out. I waited for the earthquake. It came. And it made me reel when it did come. He was actually promoted to captain in the marching regiment! Better men grow old and gray in the service before they climb to a height like that. And who could ever have known that they would make him a captain—think of it! I thought my hair would turn white.

Consider what I did—I who so loved peace and inaction. I said to myself, I am responsible to the country for this, and I must go along with him, and protect the country against him as far as I can. So I took my small amount of savings and went with a sigh and bought a place in his regiment, and away we went to the field.

And there—oh, dear, it was awful. Blunder?—why, he never did anything *but* blunder. But, you see, nobody knew the fellow's secret. No one saw him clearly; therefore, it was impossible for anyone to interpret his actions correctly. People took his idiotic blunders for performances of genius. They did, honestly! His mildest blunders were enough to make a man in his right mind cry; and they did make me cry and rage, privately. Every fresh blunder he made always improved his already fine reputation! I kept saying to myself, he'll get so high that when discovery finally does come, it will be like the sun falling out of the sky.

He went right along up, from grade to grade, over the dead bodies of his superiors, until at last, in the hottest moment of the battle—down went our colonel, and my heart jumped into my mouth, for Scoresby was next in rank! Now we're in for it, said I; we'll all be dead in ten minutes, for sure.

The battle was awfully hot; the allies were steadily giving way all over the field. Our regiment occupied a key position; a blunder now must be destruction. At this important moment, what does this fool do but move the regiment from its place and order a charge over a neighboring hill where there wasn't a suggestion of an enemy! "There you go!" I said to myself; "this *is* the end at last."

And away we did go, and we were over the shoulder of the hill before the insane movement could be discovered and stopped. And what did we find? An entire and unsuspected Russian army in reserve! And what happened? We were eaten up? That is necessarily what would have happened in ninety-nine cases out of a hundred. But no; those Russians argued that no single regiment would come wandering around there at such a time. It must be the entire English army, and that the sly Russian game was discovered and blocked; so they turned tail; and away they went, in all directions, over the hill and down into the field, in wild confusion, and we after them. They themselves broke the solid Russian center in the field, and tore through, and in no time there was the most tremendous rout of the Russians you ever saw, while the defeat of the allies was turned into a sweeping and splendid victory! His superior commander looked on with astonishment, admiration, and delight; and sent right off for Scoresby, and hugged him, and decorated him on the field in the presence of all the armies!

And what was Scoresby's blunder that time? Merely the mistaking of his right hand for his left—that was all. An order had come to him to fall back and support our right; and instead, he fell *forward* and went over the hill to the left. But the name he won that day as a marvelous military genius filled the world with his glory, and that glory will never fade while history books last.

He is just as good and sweet and lovable and unpretending as a man can be, but he doesn't know enough to come in when it rains. Now that is absolutely true. He is the greatest fool in the universe; and until half an hour ago nobody knew it but himself and me. He has been pursued, day by day and year by year, by a most amazing luckiness. He has been a shining soldier in all our wars for a generation; he has littered his whole military life with blunders, and yet has never committed one that didn't make him a knight or a baron or a lord or something. Look at his breast; why he is just clothed in medals and decorations. Well, sir, every one of them is a record of some stupidity or other; and, taken together, they are proof that the very best thing in all this world that can befall a man is to be born lucky. I say again, as I said at the dinner, Scoresby's an absolute fool.

The Wonderful Laser

by John Rangel

What can cut a diamond, shoot a pencil-thin beam of light a hundred miles, and save a life?

They can cut a pattern into metal or glass. They can change the shape of an eye and fix poor vision. They can create extremely focused heat. They can travel great distances in a perfectly straight line. They can scan a bar code in an instant and speed you through a checkout line. They are used in dentists' drills, diamond cutters, CD players, computers, remote-controlled televisions, and telephone systems. They have dozens of military uses. Quite simply, they have changed the way things work. The people who invented them have won Nobel prizes, and labs spend billions of dollars to improve and test them.

So just what are these scientific wonders? They're lasers.

But what exactly is a laser? *Laser* is an invented word. It's made up of the first letters of a long scientific term: "Light Amplification[1] by Stimulated Emission of Radiation." Basically, lasers work through a process by which light is created in a controlled way. When we think of light, we generally think of a lamp or the beam of a flashlight. But a laser's light is entirely different. And that difference starts at the level of the atom.

From a scientific point of view, you can't emphasize the atom enough. Every single thing on this planet is composed of atoms. In fact, there are only 100 different kinds of atoms in our universe. All matter, whether in the form of a raisin, a chair, a cloud, or a bubble, is made of atoms that are connected and combined in different ways.

Each atom has a central part, called a nucleus. A cloud of electrons surrounds the nucleus and moves around it in different orbits. If you imagine a group of children running around a room at different speeds and in different directions, you can picture the way electrons normally move. The atom itself is constantly moving and vibrating as well.

What scientists discovered is that directing a source of energy, such as heat, at an atom makes the electrons inside the atom get excited. When excited, they move faster and faster. But electrons always want to return to their normal state. And when they do, they release particles of energy, which take the form of light. Those released particles are called photons. To make a laser, scientists needed to control how photons are released from electrons in an atom. Scientists found that they could control the timing, the direction, and the speed of the electrons. They could stimulate the electrons to release their photons all at the same time. And they could increase the rate and power of those photons. In other words, they could create an amplification of the light.

What makes a laser a laser? For one thing, laser light travels in a straight line. It's often a line about as thick as an ordinary pencil. In some cases, it can travel for miles. And that very focused, small beam of light is different from regular light. Regular light—what we call white light—is actually a number of different colors, which we can see if that light breaks up into a rainbow. Each color represents light traveling at a certain speed. Fast light is red; slow light is blue. When white light hits a raindrop, or an ornamental crystal, for instance, it's forced to bend—as if around a corner. When it bends, the light divides into colors we can see with the naked eye.

Scientists discovered that by controlling the rate at which energy was released by electrons, they also controlled the color of the light. When electrons get excited at the same time and return to their original, or ground, state at the same time, they release the same color of light. Scientists also perfected a way to keep all the light moving in the same direction. They contain the atoms in a certain kind of material—in some cases a ruby rod, in others, a gas—called a "lasing medium." Then they wrap that container with

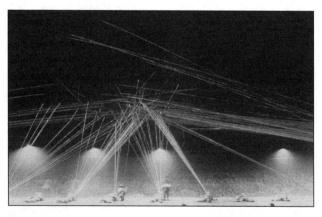

The Wonderful Laser

another material and add a series of mirrors. That way they control every single step of the process. Controlling that entire process is called a "Stimulated Emission."

An expert could spend years understanding the process by which different lasers work. But what is significant to an ordinary person is that lasers have become a part of our modern world. Lasers perform complicated jobs that ordinary hands and tools just can't do. But lasers are older than you might think. The first laser, which was built in 1960, used a rod made out of a ruby as the lasing medium. To create the laser process, a flash tube was wrapped around the rod. The electrons inside the ruby rod were "pumped" to their excited state when the flash tube filled the rod with fast beats, or pulses, of light— faster than the electrons were moving. This laser produced a powerful, pulsing red light. The scientists involved in developing that laser (among them Arthur L. Schawlow, D.F. Nelson, and R.J. Collins) were able to send this pulsing light 25 miles— between their laboratory at Bell Labs, in Murray Hill, New Jersey, and the laboratory at Bell Labs in Crawford Hill, New Jersey. The light they produced was more than a million times brighter than the sun. Imagine looking up into the sky one night and seeing a red line of light stretching for miles! To many people, lasers were unbelievable.

Once something is invented, however, people will always try to improve on it. Four years after Schawlow, Nelson, and Collins developed their ruby laser, another Bell Labs scientist, Kumar Patel, invented a carbon dioxide laser. The carbon dioxide laser was soon used in surgery in much the same way as a scalpel, or surgical knife. Now lasers are routinely used in surgeries, lowering the risk and discomfort patients go through in operations. Eye surgeons are able to save people's eyesight by repairing tears in parts of the eye. With the aid of a computer, the surgeon can point the laser with great precision. And unlike even the best surgeon's knife, lasers are completely steady. Skin doctors use lasers to repair damage done to skin through injury, aging, or too much sunbathing. Lasers can even be used to erase tattoos. Dentists have started using lasers to clean gums and teeth, as well as to fill cavities and treat infections.

And it isn't only in the field of medicine that lasers have changed our lives. A laser can serve as a hundred-mile-long tape measure, providing engineers with a pinpoint reading for their plans. Lasers can also be used to calculate distance and angles in order to build a bridge, a building, or a spaceship. Lasers can guide military weapons to specific targets, which reduces the amount of damage done to surrounding areas. When we turn on a DVD player or a CD player, we're seeing or hearing information that a laser reads as a coded message; that message is translated into sights and sounds. When you are in a checkout line at the supermarket, your items are passed through a laser, which reads the bar code on the item and translates the information into a price. Lasers can even cut precise patterns into metal and shave tiny measurements off diamonds, the hardest material known.

Go to a big rock concert, and chances are you'll see a laser light show throwing beams of colored light in all directions in time to the beat of the music. Go to an amusement park, and you may find kids playing laser tag. We even talk by laser. In the 1970s, when scientists developed tubes of glass as thin as a strand of hair, communications companies began working to send lasers along these tubes as telephone signals. Now information can travel through this system, known as "fiber optics."[2]

By now, most people take lasers for granted. But scientists are always looking for ways to make lasers better. We may someday drive cars with the aid of laser-guided systems, or cook with lasers, or heat our homes with them. In the 1950s, science fiction stories and comic books often showed astronauts meeting brutal deaths by giant "death ray" lasers. Many early critics said that lasers would be used as deadly weapons. In fact, lasers have proved to be an extremely useful invention. As with many inventions of our time, the more we use them and know about them, the better they'll get. As remarkable as the laser is today, there's no telling what amazing things it will be used for in the future.

[1] amplification: the act or result of making something bigger by enlarging or extending it

[2] fiber optics: the sending of light signals through very thin glass tubes, or fibers

Deep Water

by William O. Douglas

Some fears can be overcome.

It had happened when I was ten or eleven years old. I had decided to learn to swim. There was a pool at the Y.M.C.A. in Yakima that offered exactly the opportunity. The Yakima River was dangerous. Mother continually warned against it, and kept fresh in my mind the details of each drowning in the river. But the Y.M.C.A. pool was safe. It was only two or three feet deep at the shallow end; and while it was nine feet deep at the other, the drop was gradual. I got a pair of water wings and went to the pool. I hated to walk naked into it and show my skinny legs. But I subdued my pride and did it.

From the beginning, however, I had a deep dislike of the water when I was in it. This started when I was three or four years old and Father took me to the beach in California. He and I stood together in the surf. I hung on to him, yet the waves knocked me down and swept over me. I was buried in water. My breath was gone. I was frightened. Father laughed, but there was terror in my heart at the overpowering force of the waves.

My introduction to the Y.M.C.A. swimming pool revived unpleasant memories and stirred childish fears. But in a little while I gathered confidence. I paddled with my new water wings, watching the other boys and trying to learn by imitating them. I did this two or three times on different days and was just beginning to feel at ease in the water when the misadventure happened.

I went to the pool when no one else was there. The place was quiet. The water was still, and the tiled bottom was as white and clean as a bathtub. I was timid about going in alone, so I sat on the side of the pool to wait for others.

I had not been there long when in came a big bruiser of a boy, probably eighteen years old. He had thick hair on his chest. He was a beautiful physical specimen, with legs and arms that showed rippling muscles. He yelled, "Hi, Skinny! How'd you like to be ducked?"

With that he picked me up and tossed me into the deep end. I landed in a sitting position, swallowed water, and went at once to the bottom. I was frightened, but not yet frightened out of my wits. On the way down I planned: When my feet hit the bottom, I would make a big jump, come to the surface, lie flat on it, and paddle to the edge of the pool.

It seemed a long way down. Those nine feet were more like ninety, and before I touched bottom, my lungs were ready to burst. But when my feet hit bottom, I summoned all my strength and made what I thought was a great spring upwards. I imagined I would bob to the surface like a cork. Instead, I came up slowly. I opened my eyes and saw nothing but water—water that had a dirty yellow tinge to it. I grew panicky. I reached up as if to grab a rope and my hands clutched only at water. I couldn't breathe—I was suffocating. I tried to yell but no sound came out. Then my eyes and nose came out of the water—but not my mouth.

I thrashed at the surface of the water, swallowed, and choked. I tried to bring my legs up, but they hung as dead weights, paralyzed and rigid. A great force was pulling me under. I screamed, but only the water heard me. I had started on the long journey back to the bottom of the pool.

I struck at the water as I went down, using all my strength as one in a nightmare fights an unbeatable force. I had lost all my breath. My lungs ached, my head throbbed. I was getting dizzy.

I went down, down, endlessly. I opened my eyes. Nothing but water with a yellow glow—dark water that one could not see through.

And then sheer terror seized me, terror that knows no understanding, terror that knows no control, terror that no one can understand who has not experienced it. I was shrieking under water. I was paralyzed under water—stiff, rigid with fear. Even the screams in my throat were frozen. Only my heart, and the pounding in my head, said that I was still alive.

And then in the midst of the terror came a touch of reason. I must remember to jump when I hit the bottom. At last I felt the tiles under me. My toes reached out as if to grab them. I jumped with everything I had.

But the jump made no difference. The water was still around me. I looked for ropes, ladders, water wings. Nothing but water. A mass of yellow water held me. Sheer terror took an even deeper hold of me, like a great charge of electricity. I shook and trembled with fright. My arms wouldn't move. My legs were lead. I tried to call for help, to call for Mother. Nothing happened.

And then, strangely, there was light, I was coming out of the awful yellow water. At least my eyes were. My nose was almost out too.

Then I started down a third time. I sucked for air and got water. The yellowish light was going out.

Then all effort ceased. I relaxed. Even my legs felt limp; and a blackness swept over my brain. It wiped out fear; it wiped out terror. There was no more panic. It was quiet and peaceful. Nothing to be afraid of. This is nice . . . to be drowsy . . . to go to sleep . . . no need to jump . . . too tired to jump . . . it's nice to be carried gently . . . to float along in space . . . tender arms around me . . . tender arms like Mother's . . . now I must go to sleep. . . .

The next I remember I was lying on my stomach beside the pool, vomiting. The boy who threw me in was saying, "But I was only fooling." Someone said, "The kid nearly died. But he'll be all right now. Let's carry him to the locker room."

Several hours later I walked home. I was weak and trembling. I shook and cried when I lay on my bed.

I couldn't eat that night. For days a haunting fear was in my heart. The slightest exertion upset me, making me wobbly in the knees and sick to my stomach.

I never went back to the pool. I feared water. I avoided it whenever I could.

A few years later when I came to know the waters of the Cascades, I wanted to get into them. And whenever I did, the terror that had seized me in the pool would come back. It would take possession of me completely. My legs would become paralyzed. Icy horror would grab my heart.

This handicap stayed with me as the years rolled by. Wherever I went, the haunting fear of the water followed me. It ruined my fishing trips; deprived me of the joy of canoeing, boating, and swimming.

I used every way I knew to overcome this fear, but it held me firmly in its grip. Finally, one October, I decided to get an instructor and learn to swim. I went to a pool and practiced five days a week, an hour each day. The instructor put a belt around me. A rope attached to the belt went through a pulley that ran on an overhead cable. He held on to the end of the rope, and we went back and forth, back and forth across the pool, hour after hour, day after day, week after week. On each trip across the pool a bit of the panic seized me. Each time the instructor relaxed his hold on the rope and I went under, some of the old terror returned and my legs froze. It was three months before the strain began to lessen. Then he taught me to put my face under water and breathe out, and to raise my nose and breathe in. I repeated the exercise hundreds of times. Bit by bit I shed part of the panic that seized me when my head went under water.

Next he held me at the side of the pool and had me kick with my legs. For weeks I did just that. At first my legs refused to work. But they gradually relaxed; and finally I could command them.

Thus, piece by piece, he built a swimmer. And when he had perfected each piece, he put them together into a complete whole. In April he said, "Now you can swim. Dive off and swim the length of the pool, crawl stroke."

I did. The instructor was finished.

But I was not. I still wondered if I would be afraid when I was alone in the pool. I tried it. I swam the length up and down. Tiny traces of the old terror would return. But now I could frown and say to that terror, "Trying to scare me, eh? Well, here's to you! Look!" And off I'd go for another length of the pool.

This went on until July. But I was still not satisfied. I was not sure that all the terror had left. So I went to the lake. I swam the crawl, breast stroke, side stroke, and back stroke. Only once did the terror return. When I was in the middle of the lake, I put my face under and saw nothing but bottomless water. The old sensation returned in miniature. I laughed and said, "Well, Mr. Terror, what do you think you can do to me?" It fled and I swam on. I had conquered my fear of water.

The Last Leaf

by O. Henry

Her life hung on by the strength of the last leaf.

At the top of a squat, three-story building in New York City, Sue and Johnsy had their studio. "Johnsy" was familiar for Joanna. One was from Maine, the other from California. They had met at Delmonico's on Eighth Street and found their common tastes in art, good food, and unusual clothing so rewarding that the joint studio resulted.

That was in May. In November a cold, unseen stranger, whom the doctors called Pneumonia, stalked about the village, touching one here and one there with his icy fingers, infecting lungs and leaving his victims weak and helpless.

Mr. Pneumonia was not what you would call a gentleman. He struck Johnsy and she lay ill, scarcely moving, on her bed, looking through her bedroom window at the blank side of the next brick house.

One morning the busy doctor invited Sue into the hallway with a shaggy, gray eyebrow.

"She has one chance in—let us say, ten," he said, as he shook down the mercury in his thermometer. "And that chance is for her to want to live. Your little lady has made up her mind that she's not going to get well."

After the doctor had gone, Sue went into the workroom and cried a napkin into pulp. Then she went into Johnsy's room with her drawing board, whistling brightly.

Johnsy's eyes were open wide. She was looking out the window and counting—counting backward.

"Twelve," she said, and a little later "eleven"; and then "ten," and "nine"; and then "eight" and "seven," almost together.

Sue looked out the window. What was there to count? There was only a bare, dreary yard to be seen, and the blank side of the brick house twenty feet away. An old, old ivy vine, twisted and decayed at the roots, climbed halfway up the brick wall. The cold breath of autumn had stricken the leaves from the vine until its branches clung, almost bare, to the crumbling bricks.

"What is it, dear?" asked Sue.

"Six," said Johnsy, in almost a whisper. "They're falling faster now. Three days ago there were almost a hundred. It made my head ache to count them. But now it's easy. There goes another one. There are only five left now."

"Five what, dear? Tell your Sudie."

"Leaves. On the ivy vine. When the last one falls I must go, too. I've known that for three days. Didn't the doctor tell you?"

"Oh, I never heard of such nonsense," complained Sue with magnificent scorn. "What have old ivy leaves to do with your getting well? Why, the doctor told me this morning that your chances for getting well real soon were—let's see exactly what he said—he said the chances where ten to one! Try to take some soup now, and let Sudie get back to her drawing."

"There goes another," said Johnsy, keeping her eyes fixed out the window. "That leaves just four. I want to see the last one fall before it gets dark. Then I'll go, too."

"Johnsy, dear," said Sue, bending over her, "will you promise me to keep your eyes closed, and not look out the window until I am done working? I need the light, or I would draw the shade down."

"Couldn't you draw in the other room?" asked Johnsy, coldly.

"I'd rather be here by you," said Sue. "Besides, I don't want you to keep looking at those silly ivy leaves."

"Tell me as soon as you have finished," said Johnsy, closing her eyes, and lying white and still as a fallen statue, "because I want to see the last one fall. I'm tired of waiting. I'm tired of thinking. I want to turn loose my hold on everything, and go sailing down, down, just like one of those poor, tired leaves."

"Try to sleep," said Sue. "I must call Behrman up to be my model for the old miner. I'll not be gone a minute. Don't try to move 'til I come back."

Old Behrman was a painter who lived on the ground floor beneath them. Behrman was a failure in art. He had been always about to paint a great work of art, a masterpiece, but had never yet begun it. He earned a little by serving as a model to those young artists who could not pay the price of a professional. He drank gin too much, and still talked of his coming masterpiece. For the rest he was a fierce little old man who criticized softness in anyone and who saw himself as protecting the two young artists in the studio above.

Sue found Behrman in his dimly lighted den below. She told him of Johnsy's fancy, and how she feared she would indeed, light and frail as a leaf herself, float away, when her slight hold upon the world grew weaker.

Old Behrman, with his red eyes plainly streaming, shouted his anger at such idiotic imaginings.

"What!" he cried. "Are there people in the world with the foolishness to die because leaves drop off from a vine? No, I will not model for your fool miner!"

"She is very ill and weak," said Sue, "and the fever has left her mind full of strange fancies. Very well, Mr. Behrman, if you do not care to model for me, you needn't. But I think you are a horrible old man."

"Who said I will not model?" yelled Behrman. "Go on—lead the way. I will come with you."

Johnsy was sleeping when they went upstairs. Sue pulled the shade down and motioned Behrman into the other room. In there they peered out the window fearfully at the ivy vine. Then they looked at each other for a moment without speaking. A cold rain was falling, mixed with snow. Behrman, in his old blue shirt, took his seat as the miner on an upturned kettle for a rock.

When Sue awoke from an hour's sleep the next morning, she found Johnsy with dull, wide-open eyes staring at the drawn green shade.

"Pull it up, I want to see," she ordered, in a whisper.

Wearily Sue obeyed.

But, lo! After the beating rain and fierce gusts of wind that had endured through the livelong night, there yet stood out against the brick wall one ivy leaf. It was the last one on the vine. Still dark green near its stem, but with its edges colored with the yellow of decay, it hung bravely from a branch some twenty feet above the ground.

"It is the last one," said Johnsy. "I thought it

would surely fall during the night. I heard the wind. It will fall today, and I shall die at the same time."

"Dear, dear!" said Sue, leaning her worn face down to the pillow, "Think of me, if you won't think of yourself. What would I do?"

But Johnsy did not answer. The lonesomest thing in all the world is a soul when it is making ready to go on its mysterious, far journey. The fancy seemed to possess her more strongly as one by one the ties that bound her to friendship and to earth were loosed.

The day wore away, and even through the twilight they could see the lone ivy leaf clinging to its stem against the wall. And then, with the coming of the night, the north wind was again loosed, while the rain still beat against the windows and dripped down from the edge of the roof.

When it was light enough, Johnsy, without mercy, commanded that the shade be raised.

The ivy leaf was still there.

Johnsy lay for a long time looking at it. And then she called to Sue, who was stirring her chicken soup over the gas stove.

"I've been a bad girl, Sudie," said Johnsy. "Something had made that last leaf stay there to show me how wicked I was. It is a sin to want to die. You may bring me a little soup now—no; bring me a hand-mirror first, and then pack some pillows about me, and I will sit up and watch you cook."

An hour later she said:

"Sudie, someday I hope to paint the Bay of Naples."

The doctor came in the afternoon, and Sue had an excuse to go into the hallway as he left.

"Even chances," said the doctor, taking Sue's thin, shaking hand in his. "With good nursing you'll win. And now I must see another case I have downstairs. Behrman, his name is—some kind of an artist, I believe. Pneumonia, too. He is an old, weak man, and the attack is a bad one. There is no hope for him; but he goes to the hospital today to be made more comfortable."

The next day the doctor said to Sue: "She's out of danger. You've won. Food and rest now—that's all."

And that afternoon Sue came to the bed where Johnsy lay, and put one arm around her, pillows and all.

"I have something to tell you, white mouse," she said. "Mr. Behrman died of pneumonia today in the hospital. He was ill only two days. The cleaning man found him on the morning of the first day in his room downstairs, helpless with pain. His shoes and clothing were wet through and icy cold. They couldn't imagine where he had been on such a dreadful night. And then they found a lantern, still lighted, and a ladder that had been dragged from its place, and some scattered brushes, and some green and yellow paints, and—look out the window, dear, at the last ivy leaf on the wall. Didn't you wonder why it never fluttered or moved when the wind blew? Ah, darling, it's Behrman's masterpiece—he painted it there the night that the last leaf fell."

What Animals Think

by Jana Martin

**Animals are smarter than we think.
Just ask them.**

The next time you hear the phrase "dumb beast," think again. For scientists are finding that animals of all kinds, from crows to parrots to chimpanzees to dogs, are smarter than we once thought. Animals, we are discovering, have their own kind of intelligence. And not only are we learning how to recognize it, we're learning how to respect it as well.

What is intelligence? We think of intelligence as the ability to communicate, the ability to problem-solve, and the ability to make decisions. Given that, are animals really intelligent?

Take the ability to communicate. What is communication? The term might be defined as a series of sounds and expressions that are made to convey a feeling or an idea. Well, you might say, that sounds like language, but animals don't have a vocabulary. But animals *do* have a vocabulary, after all.

Let's start with a caged bird you might find in a pet shop, such as an African Gray parrot. Twenty years ago, a researcher named Irene Pepperberg at the University of Arizona decided to test a theory. Her theory was that while we might think parrots were only capable of imitating human speech—as in, "Polly want a cracker"— in reality, parrots can actually understand the meaning of speech, too.

For her study, Pepperberg worked with an African Gray parrot named Alex, as well as other birds of the species. Pepperberg created a series of tests and exercises that built up Alex's vocabulary. But what each term meant to the parrot was up to him. In time, Alex learned the names of more than 40 objects. If Pepperberg said, "Where's the cup, Alex?" Alex would point at the cup. If Pepperberg said, "Where's the ball?" Alex could tell the difference between a ball and another toy and point to the ball.

Alex could also understand concepts. He understood the ideas of *same* and *different*. He could distinguish between large and small objects. Pepperberg and Alex worked on tasks, like "Show me the same size balls," or "What's the big size? What's the little size?" Alex showed that parrots can think. So much for the idea of a birdbrain!

Alex showed that a parrot isn't just imitating humans when it talks—it's actually communicating. And he proved that he was not just hearing sounds when people spoke to him—he was actually listening and understanding. Other animals have shown that they can solve problems and have changed the standards by which we distinguish humans from other creatures. With their help, and the research being done throughout the world, we have entered the era of animal intelligence.

Before Jane Goodall began studying primates such as chimpanzees and orangutans, it was commonly thought that we human beings proved our superior intelligence through our use of tools. Early humans used rocks to sharpen spears and to pound fruit or meat. Eventually, humans developed all the basic tools we use today: the spear, the pencil, the shovel, the knife, the wheel. But in the 1960s, Goodall discovered that humans aren't the only mammals to use tools. She observed chimpanzees around a termite mound. Inside the mound were hundreds of termites, which chimps like to eat. How would the hungry chimps get to those insects, Goodall wondered. Then one chimp found a stick on the ground and picked it up. First the chimp trimmed the edge of it with its teeth, and then—to Goodall's amazement—stuck it into a hole in the mound and fished out a termite. Pretty soon the entire band of chimps was feasting on the bugs out of the mound.

At first, most of the scientific community did not believe Goodall's observations. They had to see for themselves. But since Goodall made her discovery and changed forever the boundaries between humans and animals, other animals have also been discovered to use tools. In New Caledonia, a remote island in the Pacific Ocean, there is a species of crow that practices its own version of bug-on-a-stick. To get out the fat grubs[1] that live underneath the bark of rotten logs, the crows use twigs to spear them. What's even more fascinating is that the crows don't just use any stick. They use only certain sticks to do the job. We still don't know what thoughts go through a crow's mind as it looks for the right stick: perhaps, is it strong enough? Is it thin enough to reach into the cracks in the bark? Is it pointed enough?

In any case, the process of selecting the right stick can also be said to be the process of making a decision, for the crow must decide which stick to use to spear the grub. Decision-making, like problem solving, is an aspect of intelligence that we humans once thought only we could master.

Take a common sight in our society: a guide dog leading a blind person. Guide dogs are trained to help blind people walk along a busy sidewalk, get on and off buses and subways, and find their way from place to place. Labrador retrievers and German shepherds are breeds that excel as guide dogs. The dog wears a special shoulder harness that allows the blind person to tell which direction the dog is going, if it's stopping, or if it's turning right or left. By leaning its weight against the blind person's legs, a guide dog can also communicate: "Hey, we need to go this way now."

The relationship between a guide dog and its blind owner is one built on trust. The owner trusts that the dog will not disobey him or her or do anything destructive. The owner trusts that when other people come near, the dog will not bark, and when on the subway, the dog will not get nervous and snap at another passenger. The owner trusts that the dog will use its training to do the right thing. Most of the time, it does.

But there are unusual times when all the training in the world can't help. In a crisis, a dog is sometimes forced to choose between its training, which says, "Obey your master," and its awareness of what's actually happening. The dog has to make a decision. It could be a matter of life and death.

Chuck L., a blind man who has been sightless since birth, says he owes his life to his guide dog Trina. Trina, a yellow Labrador retriever, was guiding Chuck down a busy street one morning, as usual. Chuck and Trina live in lower Manhattan, where Chuck works in the world of finance. They usually move quickly through crowds, and this day was no different. Chuck can tell the length of a block and says he can always feel Trina slowing down at the curb before she stops for a traffic signal.

But that September morning, Trina suddenly stopped dead in her tracks. Chuck wanted to keep moving, as it was nearly 9 A.M. and he wanted to get to the office. Trina stood still. She would not move. "She wasn't being defiant," Chuck said, "she wasn't trying to disobey me. But she wanted me to understand that she couldn't, and wouldn't, do what I was asking." Chuck pulled on the harness and spoke sharply to her. He could feel the normal rush of people walking past them. He could picture Trina and himself standing in the middle of a street crowded with people, blocking their way. Chuck was getting nervous.

Trina would not budge. A few more seconds went by. Trina began to growl in a low tone. She was snorting, as if there were a strange smell in the air. But Chuck could feel nothing. And when Chuck tried to pull her along, she very clearly turned and stood so he could not get past her solid body. Then, just as firmly, she turned and headed them back for home.

Chuck recalls that he decided he had to trust his dog. "She knew something I didn't," he said. Whether she saw it, or sensed it, who can say? But Trina walked as fast as Chuck could follow, determined to get back inside their home as soon as possible. In fact, Chuck says, Trina actually nosed his legs forward as he got inside the building—even as she was maneuvering her body to get inside both lobby doors. At one point he tripped, and she valiantly helped him regain his footing by placing herself underneath him so he could lean on her.

It wasn't a moment too soon. That morning was September 11, 2001, and Chuck had been headed on the half-mile walk to the World Trade Center, where he worked. They were already safely back home when the planes hit. Somehow, Chuck thinks, Trina sensed something was wrong and refused to do her usual job. "She had clearly made a decision that her understanding of the situation was stronger than mine," he later said. But it took a lot of thought. She had to sense something was wrong and then figure out how to convince Chuck to believe her and follow her. It took a lot of bravery, and it saved their lives.

There are examples of animal intelligence everywhere, among nearly every species—we just need to know where to look and what to look for. In Africa, the meerkat, a small mammal that lives in the ground, has a language that includes different warning calls for different predators, from snakes to eagles. In other words, the meerkat can tell the difference between one predator and the other and communicate it to its fellow meerkats. And those meerkats know what the warning is saying. That's more than instinct at work, say animal behavior experts: that's intelligence.

---

[1] grubs: worm-like larva of certain beetles and other insects

child
OF ALL AGES

by P. J. Plauger

Here is the story of a child who refused to grow up.

The child sat in the waiting room with her hands folded neatly on her lap. She sat very still and erect.

She looked as if she had done a lot of waiting. May Foster drew back from the two-way mirror through which she had been studying her newest problem. She always felt a little guilty about spying on children like this before an interview, but she felt it helped her handle cases better.

May stepped out of the closet where the mirror was hidden and returned to her desk.

"Louise, you can bring in the child now," she said to her secretary.

The girl glanced about the room, then marched up to the visitor's chair and planted herself in it with a thump. "My name is Melissa," she said, adding a

Reprinted by permission of the author. Copyright © 1975 by P. J. Plauger. First appeared in *Analog Science Fiction/Science Fact*.

nervous grin. She was all little girl now, squirming and kicking one shoe against another.

May shook herself. She couldn't believe it. Melissa looked more like a model eight-year-old than a constant troublemaker going on, what was it? Fourteen. *Fourteen*?

"You've been suspended from school for the third time this year, Melissa," she said sternly.

"Yep," the child said with no trace of regret.

"Do you want to tell me about it?" May asked.

"What's to say? Old Man M—uh, Mr. Morrisey and I got into another argument in history class." She giggled. "He had to pull rank on me to win. Do you know what he was trying to palm off on the class? He was trying to say that the Industrial Revolution in England was a step backward. Kids working seven days a week, fourteen hours at a stretch, just to earn a few pennies a week. He never thought to ask *why* they did it."

"You talk as if you were there," May said. "Even if you were right, you still could have been more polite, you know. I suspect your problem isn't just with school. How are things going at home?"

"Home." Her tone was bitter. "My fa—my foster father died last year. Heart attack. Bam! Mrs. Stuart still hasn't gotten over it."

"And you?" May prodded.

"Everyone dies, sooner or later. I wish Mr. Stuart had hung around a while longer, though. He was OK." Melissa sounded genuinely saddened.

"And your mother?" May asked.

"My foster mother can't wait for me to grow up

and let her off the hook. Jeez, she'd marry me off next month if the law allowed. She keeps dragging boys home to take me out." Her voice was harsh.

"Do you like going out with boys, Melissa?"

"Some. I mean boys are OK. I mean I don't hate boys or anything. I mean I've still got lots of time for that sort of stuff when I grow up."

"You are fourteen, Melissa."

There was a moment of silence.

"Mrs. Foster, do you read science fiction?"

"Uh, some."

"Well, what do you think of it? I mean do you enjoy it?"

"Well, uh, I guess I like some of it. My husband reads it mostly. And my father-in-law. He's a chemist," May added lamely, as though that excused something.

"Mrs. Foster, what would you say if I told you my father was a wizard?"

"Frankly, I'd say you'd built up an elaborate story about your unknown parents. Orphans often do, you know."

"Thanks for being honest. I suspect, however, you are willing to believe that I might be more than your average troublemaker."

May could do nothing but nod.

"What would you say," Melissa whispered, "if I told you I was over twenty-four hundred years old?"

May felt surprise, fear, and an emotion that had no name. "I'd say that you ought to meet my husband."

The child sat at the dinner table with her hands folded neatly on her lap. The three adults made conversation. Melissa answered questions but never volunteered any small talk of her own.

George Foster Jr. sensed that the seemingly innocent child sitting across from him was waiting them out. One thing he was sure of was that if this child were indeed twenty-four hundred years old, he was in no position to outwit her.

George tried to draw her out. "May tells me you were in England for a while."

"I didn't actually say so, but yes I was. Actually, what Mrs. Foster and I discussed was the Industrial Revolution."

"And your father was a magician?" May did not want the subject changed.

"Not a magician, a wizard." Melissa was fed up. "He didn't practice magic or cast spells; he was a wise man, a scholar. You could call him a scientist, except there wasn't too much science back then. Not that he didn't know a lot about some things— obviously he did—but he didn't work with an organized body of knowledge the way people do now. Anyway, he was working on a method of restoring youth. Everybody was, in those days. Very popular!"

"You mean, you know how to reverse aging?" George Sr. asked.

"Sorry, no, I didn't say that. I only know of one man who did that. For a while. But he didn't tell anyone else how he did it, as far as I know. The knowledge died with him. My father's only real success story was me. He found a way to stop the aging process before I became an adult."

"Could you describe the method?" George Sr. asked.

"I could, but I won't. It doesn't work for adults. I've tried. Perhaps I am just a product of my age, but keeping it a secret seems to be the only way to protect myself. I've had a few painful experiences."

Child of All Ages

"Why have you told us all this, Melissa?" George Sr. wondered out loud.

"Isn't it obvious?" She folded her hands on her lap in that usual way. "I'm telling you all about myself because it's time to move on again. I've overstayed my welcome with the Stuarts. I thought it might be easier this time to take the honest approach."

"You mean, you want us to help you get into a new foster home?" George Jr. asked.

"George, don't be so thickheaded," May said. "Don't you understand? She's asking us to take her in."

Since George Sr. and May thought it was the best answer, George Jr. found himself smiling at his new daughter, who was crying tears of happiness.

The child sat under the tree with her hands folded neatly on her lap. She looked up as George Sr. approached. His step had grown less confident in the last year; the stiffness and uncertainty of old age could no longer be ignored.

"Hello, Grandpa," Melissa said.

"Mortimer died," was all he said.

"I was afraid he might. He lived a long time, for a white rat."

They sat in silence, Melissa as patient as ever.

"You could give me some of your formula," George Sr. said.

"No."

"I know you have some to spare. You come here to the woods to make it, don't you?"

"I told you it wouldn't help you any, and you promised not to ask," Melissa stated simply.

Child of All Ages   **85**

"Wouldn't you like to grow up, sometime? Don't you mind wasting time in school? Learning the same things over and over again?"

"What waste? Time? Got lots of that. How much of your life have you spent actually doing research, compared to the time spent writing reports and driving to work? How much time does Mrs. Foster get to spend talking to troubled kids? She's lucky if she averages five minutes a day. We all spend most of our time doing ordinary chores. It would be unusual if any of us did not. I'll stick with what I've got.

"I'm sorry, Grandpa. I really am. I couldn't help Mortimer and I can't help you. I can't help any of you."

The child sat in the pew with her hands folded neatly on her lap. She could hear the cold rain lash against the stained glass windows.

Her time with the Fosters was over. Even with the conflict at the end, she was able to look back over her stay with fond memories.

Things began to go really sour after George Sr. had his first mild stroke. George Jr. could not believe she would do nothing to help. There was nothing she could say or do to lessen the strain. Just being there, healthy and still a child, unchanged in five years— her very presence made a mockery of the old man's steady retreat from life.

May envied the child her second chance at the beauty she fancied lost with the passing of youth.

George Sr. suffered a second stroke.

May was furious—there was no talking to her. George Jr. could think only of his father's approaching death. Melissa went to her room, thought things over, and prepared to leave. As she crept out the back door, she heard George Jr. talking about her on the phone. It sounded as if he was trying to talk some officials into coming over to investigate her.

She hot-wired a neighbor's car and set off for town. Cars were pulling into the Foster's drive as she went past. She had not left a minute too soon.

"We have to close up soon," a soft voice said behind her. "It's nearly midnight. You should be getting home."

Melissa smiled at the priest. "I just came in to get out of the rain. I'll be on my way now, Father."

She walked out of the church into the rain, knowing that she would have to find shelter for the night. Up ahead, on the other side of the street, a movie theater's sign splashed light through the drizzle. Black letters spelled out a greeting:

****

WALT DISNEY TRIPLE FEATURE
CONTINUOUS PERFORMANCES
FOR CHILDREN OF ALL AGES

****

"That's me," Melissa decided. She crossed the street and stepped up to the ticket window. Leaving rain and cold behind for a time, she plunged gratefully into the warm darkness.

Martial Arts

by Barbara Seiger

It's more than a means of self-defense. It's a way of life.

Does the name Bruce Lee mean anything to you? Or Jackie Chan? Or Jet Li? Chances are their names ring a bell. Maybe you've seen these men in a movie or read about them or heard about them. They're the guys who strike out with the speed of a laser and move with the grace of a dancer. They jump, chop, and jab. They grunt. They hurtle. They destroy their enemies. They're action figures right out of a comic strip. But they're real men. They're also martial artists.

The term *martial arts* means war skills, that is, the skills soldiers acquire and use when they attack an enemy or defend themselves when they are attacked. The origins of martial arts go back to the tenth century, a time known as "the Golden Age of the Samurai," the famous Japanese warriors.

But physical fitness and mastery of weapons is only half of the story.

All martial arts students understand that the brain rules the body. Therefore, a martial artist must also develop mental control and concentration. Martial artists have to learn to hold their temper, to think before they move, and to make quick decisions in order to overcome their enemies. The consequence of making the wrong judgment can be serious.

It is interesting, therefore, that at the same time people were using martial arts to fight, another kind of martial art was developing. People who studied this art weren't soldiers; they were ordinary people who realized that if they wanted to improve their lives, they also had to discipline their minds and bodies. They did it by playing a martial arts game in which two opponents follow a set pattern of rules in a contest of will and strength. This game is also a kind of fight, but without a negative outcome. It is not a fight to the death. Today, many martial arts schools follow the old traditions and teach martial arts as a way to protect and defend; however, the tradition of game playing also continues.

JUDO

Judo, which literally means "gentleness practice," had its beginning in the ancient Japanese art of *jujutsu*, a system of hand-to-hand combat.

The founder of modern judo, Dr. Jigoro Kano (1860–1938) had studied jujutsu as a young man. But as he grew older, he taught himself to use jujutsu techniques in a different way. He realized he could win by using the energy of his opponent rather than his own energy. Dr. Kano modified the practice of jujutsu. He called his art *judo*, and he set up a school to teach it.

Judo is unique because it does not rely on strength to overcome an opponent. Its basic strategy is one of nonresistance. In judo, the athlete tries to get an opponent off balance in order to throw, trip, choke, or hold him or her. Judo also uses many techniques that give a small opponent an advantage over a larger, stronger opponent. Judo has hundreds of moves, and every movement has a definite meaning and purpose. The moves fall into three general categories: throwing an opponent's body; pinning or locking an opponent's body; injuring an opponent. Each of these tactics can take years to master.

Mastering judo can actually beautify a person's life. Judo students learn a code of behavior that helps them move from *jutsu* (martial art) to *do* (way of life). *Do's* two main principles are to be honest and to behave well at all times. In fact, a student who does anything that might bring shame to the school must leave.

There are two main types of judo: *randori*, or free competition, and *kata*, in which two people practice the exercises together but do not compete with each other. One American kind of judo uses hand-to-hand fighting. This involves some aspects of boxing and wrestling but has no real connection to the art of judo.

Judo matches in the United States may either take place during a limited period of time or last until one of the two opponents wins a point. The athlete can win in a number of ways: by throwing an opponent to the ground; by paralyzing an opponent in a certain position for a certain amount of time; or by forcing an opponent to give up through special holds or arm locks. Judo opponents are not allowed to kick, hit, or attack the eyes.

AIKIDO

Modern *aikido* was developed by Master Morihei Ueshiba (1883–1969), also known as *O-Sensei*, the Great Teacher. A small but strong and powerful man—he was 5'2" and weighed a solid 180 pounds—Ueshiba mastered *aiki-jujutsu*, a violent approach to the martial arts that focuses on destroying one's enemy, and transformed it into *aiki-do*, a way to resolve conflict that focuses on character and behavior. Ueshiba, like other great martial arts masters, understood that he had to move beyond *aiki-jujutsu*. He knew he must achieve harmony with all things at all times, that is, harmony with the universe. He also understood that when one feels this harmony, there is no longer any enemy. Ueshiba called this new martial art *aikido*. In his own words:

> ...*I have grown to feel that the whole earth is my house and that the sun, the moon and the stars are all my own. I have freed myself from all desire, not only for position, fame, and property, but also the desire to be strong....I set my mind on budo[1] when I was about fifteen....But there was no one to instruct me in the essence of budo...I finally understood... budo is not about defeating your opponents by force, nor is it a tool to lead the world into destruction with weapons....True budo is to nourish life and foster peace, love, and respect, not to blast the world to pieces with weapons.*

Here is an interesting fact: The Yoshinkan Aikido school in Tokyo, established by Ueshiba's student, Gozo Shioda, provides aikido teachers for all of the 40,000 Tokyo metropolitan police.

CAPOEIRA

Capoeira was created by Africans who were brought to Brazil as slaves four hundred years ago. When the Dutch and Portuguese in Brazil were fighting, many slaves ran away and hid in the forests where they gathered in villages. Because the former slaves knew they would have to fight to keep their freedom, capoeira began with fighting moves.

For a long time, most capoeira fighters were criminals who were expert in the use of kicks and head-butts, as well as in the use of blade weapons. Sometimes tough capoeira fighters led bands through the streets and fought with other bands.

In the 1930s, two capoeira schools opened and that changed everything. From that time on, capoeira was taught to children of the upper classes and practiced openly.

While capoeira is a martial art, it is also *jogo*, a game and a social event for people of all ages. The game has many purposes—among them to develop sound minds and bodies and to learn how to defend oneself. These purposes are similar to most martial arts; however, capoeira has several special elements that other martial arts do not share.

First, songs play a big part in the way *jogo* is played. The type of game to be played (fast or slow, friendly or tough) depends upon the kind of music being played.

Different rhythms call for a different speed and a different type of game. The words of the songs, usually in Portuguese, also affect the way the game is played.

Second, the players' movements are different from other kinds of martial arts. The game begins with musicians playing instruments such as the *berimbau* (one string played with a bow), *atabaque* (conga drum), *pandiero* (tambourine) and *agoga* (bell). Players kneel and form a circle or *roda*. Then two players enter the circle, usually by doing a cartwheel. Once inside, the players jump, kick, flip, and do handstands either separately or together. Think athletic disco dancing!

Today, capoeira is spreading rapidly to other countries largely because of its great appeal. Like no other martial art, capoeira is a means of fighting *and* a dance, and it is performed to music whose strong rhythms make it almost irresistible.

KARATE

The word *karate* is a combination of two Japanese characters: *kara*, meaning "empty," and *te*, meaning

"hand." Thus, karate means "empty hand." But this empty hand is a powerful weapon. Karate students toughen their hands and feet by hitting objects and/or driving their hands into sand and gravel. The art involves striking an opponent with the hands, elbows, knees, and feet. By aiming at sensitive places like the throat and temple, the karate expert can kill with a single blow, so he or she uses this skill only in an emergency.

Karate, like the other martial arts, is a total way of life that goes beyond self-defense. Thus, by mastering karate, people improve themselves. For example, getting rid of weak movements in karate helps people get rid of weak thinking. It also works the other way: Strong thoughts help to make the karate stronger.

Is martial arts for you? That depends. If you just want to learn a few good moves to be a better fighter, forget it. Go take some boxing lessons. Better yet, resolve your conflicts in nonviolent ways. You might even try to turn your enemies into friends.

On the other hand, if you're serious and you want to develop your body and your mind, then studying one of the martial arts might be something for you to consider. There are a lot of schools out there, so you will have many to choose from. But be careful. The only "art" some people are interested in is the art of taking your money, so before you choose a school, talk to some of the teachers. Talk to some of the students. Observe a class. Try to get a feel for the place. You'll know when it's right for you. Then practice, practice, practice, and master every task you're given. A year from now, you might be the person you always wanted to be.

[1] Budo: the martial way

Katherine **Dunham**

Dance legend with a mission

by Lynn Norment

**She brought together a community with her love
for dance and different cultures.**

Like a precious stone glistening in a pile of rocks,
the Katherine Dunham Museum and Children's
Workshop stands on the corner of Tenth Street and
Pennsylvania Avenue, surrounded by poverty and
the run-down conditions of East St. Louis, Illinois.
In that way, it is a fitting tribute to its founder,
Katherine Dunham, the legendary dancer, choreographer,[1] anthropologist,[2] and writer.

Born in Joliet, Illinois, Dunham grew up with her
father, stepmother, and older brother. Her father ran
a dry cleaning business, but his first love was music.
In the evenings while Katherine played the piano,
her father and brother played along on their instruments. Katherine learned to dance at an early age. By
the time she was eight, she had raised money for the
church by staging a musical production.

When she graduated from high school, Katherine

decided that she wanted to continue her studies. She entered the University of Chicago and formed a dancing school to earn her way through college. The school was in a cold and drafty barn. It took some lively dancing to save teacher and students from catching cold, but they shivered and sneezed their way through.

It was while she was at the University of Chicago that Ms. Dunham developed an interest in anthropology. She wanted to study the different cultures that had their roots in Africa. She wanted to record dance styles and the other ways people had of expressing themselves. At the University of Chicago, Ms. Dunham

so impressed the Rosenwald Foundation with her enthusiasm to learn various dance forms and with her success in her courses that it gave her money to do research in five Caribbean countries.

She lived in tiny villages in those countries and spent her time watching and joining in dances and ceremonies never before seen by outsiders. Once she got caught taking pictures of a secret ritual, or religious ceremony, but was lucky enough to escape any punishment.

When she got to Haiti, Ms. Dunham became interested in voodoo, a religion that affects the everyday lives of the Haitians. The people who had been brought to Haiti from Africa had combined their many different religions into one, which became known as voodoo. It dealt with love, birth, sickness, death, legal disputes, and money.

Voodoo makes us think of mysterious happenings, magic spells, and secret formulas. The word itself probably came from an African word for "godlike" or "set apart and holy." Today, just as when Ms. Dunham recorded her experiences, voodoo is concerned with rituals in which little-understood forces can be directed for good or evil. Voodoo also involves communicating with the ghosts of the dead and understanding the relationship between the living and the dead.

Ms. Dunham became so involved in the culture of Haiti that she was allowed to go through elaborate training in order to take part in the sacred voodoo ceremonies. She was on her way to becoming a voodoo priestess.

Ms. Dunham was interested in voodoo because she was an anthropologist. She gained insight into the culture by watching and recording its ceremonies, among them, rituals to heal the sick. In a typical healing ceremony, a shallow hole in the shape of a grave would be prepared. Three pints of rainwater and three pints of red wine would be placed in the hole. The ground around it would be decorated with cornmeal in a checkerboard pattern. Then a mat would be placed over the hole and a stake driven in at one end. The sick person then lay down on the mat. A rooster was placed between his or her knees and covered with a white sheet. The priest or priestess then sprinkled salt on the sheet. Twenty-one white candles in groups of seven were placed on the ground. When an hour had passed, the rooster was removed and it was believed that the sick person was made well because the rooster had absorbed all the illness.

An anthropologist might draw the parallel to our own culture, in which a doctor tells a person who has no particular illness to take two aspirin and go to bed. Sometimes the person feels fine the next morning. The technique works on the mind. The person feels well because he or she believes in the power of the aspirin.

Ms. Dunham was also interested in voodoo because she was a dancer and choreographer. The rituals that the Haitians held to please the gods inspired her to create new dances. She listened as the drums, a sacred and essential part of the ritual, roused the excitement of the people. The drummers had learned a great many rhythms and songs. They also needed enormous energy. The drums continued to beat through the night; the dancers became more and more excited. Ms. Dunham brought that same sense of excitement to her musical productions.

The fact that the Haitians allowed Katherine Dunham to take part in their mysterious practices, which include the use of magic, demonstrated the trust and belief that they had in her.

Ms. Dunham created a revolution in modern dance in the 1940s and 1950s by introducing movements that were influenced by the tribal dances she had seen while studying different cultures. She herself performed in these original productions, and she wore costumes inspired by tribal clothing. As a performer, she was bursting with energy. As a choreographer, she created dances that brought the rhythms and the excitement of the tribal dances home to the audiences. She had danced her way through hardship and discouragement to success.

In the midst of the civil rights uprisings of the 1960s, the already well-known and highly respected Ms. Dunham was asked by Southern Illinois University to establish and direct its Performing Arts Training Center in East St. Louis. She accepted the offer and planned to move there.

On the very day she arrived in East St. Louis, she was arrested because she had protested the arrest of black students. University officials criticized her for being friendly with protesters and suggested that she move to the Carbondale, Illinois, campus. "I'm here now, and this is where I'll stay," the strong-willed Ms. Dunham announced. "There were disturbances going on all the time," she recalls, "and I decided to direct some of that energy into something useful."

That "something useful" at first was the University's Performing Arts and Training Center and later her own museum and dance school. "We had a very hard time at first teaching young men to dance, because they thought it absurd," she says. "But when we brought in drummers from Africa and the Caribbean and began to teach about the tribal war ceremonies, a lot more interest developed."

Ms. Dunham is no longer able to dance as she did so well during her performing career. She walks slowly now and needs the assistance of a cane. Still, she takes great pleasure and pride in overseeing youngsters from the East St. Louis area as they learn and perform the Dunham Technique of Dance. In a coach house behind the museum, children ages six through twelve come after school to take dance lessons. They perform for audiences at various schools and for programs given to benefit charity. Attired in Caribbean and African costumes, the young performers dance to the rhythms of "African drums," which are played by the students.

Katherine Dunham has had a positive influence on the mostly black community of East St. Louis, a city of fifty thousand that was almost completely destroyed by uprisings in the 1960s. In that time, the whites living there and successful businessmen abandoned the city, making the problem worse for the blacks who were left behind.

Darryl Braddix, an East St. Louis firefighter and former dancer who is the manager of the dance workshop, gives credit to Ms. Dunham for rescuing him from the streets. "If it was not for her, I would probably be in jail," he says. Braddix was eighteen when Ms. Dunham first met him and helped get him started.

That Katherine Dunham would settle in East St. Louis is no surprise to those who have followed the life and career of this talented woman, who has given so much to her community and to the world of dance.

Ms. Dunham's long and exciting career has taken her from modest beginnings in Chicago and Joliet, Illinois, to the Caribbean, Africa, and other parts of the world, and now back to Illinois.

She has starred in and arranged dances for Broadway productions, Hollywood films, and television shows. She has written books, among them an autobiography of the early part of her life, an account of her experiences in Jamaica, and the story of her introduction to voodoo in her beloved second home, Haiti. She has published many articles on her twin interests, anthropology and dance. She has also been the subject of many books by well-known authors. Without question, Katherine Dunham has made an enormous contribution to the arts.

In 1983 she was among five distinguished artists honored at a Kennedy Center banquet and a White House gathering hosted by the President. In addition, her life and art have been captured in several television specials. The famous choreographer, Alvin Ailey, has worked with Ms. Dunham to stage and film her major productions.

Even though she has received all this praise, Katherine Dunham's greatest joy these days comes not from the numerous honors but from the East St. Louis youngsters who are learning much of her vast knowledge of dance. Her greatest accomplishment, she says, is "breaking through various social obstacles." As everyone who knows her maintains, the Katherine Dunham Technique is more than just dance—it is a way of life.

---

[1] choreographer: someone who arranges the steps for stage dance
[2] anthropologist: someone who is an expert in anthropology, which is the study of human cultures

Cleaning Up
The Environment

By Lesley A. DuTemple

Keeping our water clean is not so easy.

People view oil spills with horror, especially when gooey oil comes ashore and fouls sparkling beaches or runs into streams and kills entire fish populations. The public wants something done immediately, and it usually demands that the mess be cleaned up and the environment restored.

Cleaning up after a large oil spill is never simple or easy, and frequently, it's not immediate. Even the best efforts often can't entirely fix the problem—the scope of most oil spills is just too large. Sometimes, the remedies employed to clean up a spill actually make the problem worse.

Because oil is essentially liquid, it travels like liquid—it can go almost anywhere. When oil is spilled in water, it can travel even more extensively because it can go wherever the water goes. Regardless of where a spill occurs, the oil may end up on sandy beaches, rocky coastlines, mingled into the reeds and bottoms of saltwater marshes, or coating the fresh-water shorelines. Every place that oil settles poses a different cleanup problem.

When oil is spilling, the first thing cleanup crews want to do is shut off the source of the oil. Sometimes, such as when the spill involves a pipeline, the spill can be stopped by simply closing a valve. But it's not so easy to stop the spill if it's coming from a damaged tanker. Sometimes a leaking hull can be patched; usually, however, the best that can be

done is for the owner of the cargo to try and save the remaining oil by transferring it onto smaller vessels. Once oil spills, cleanup crews are first concerned with containing the spill as much as possible.

Booms

If oil is spreading slowly, seas are calm, and cleanup crews act quickly, some of the spilled oil can be recovered, sometimes before it does much damage. Tubes or poles, called booms, are linked together and placed around the edges of the spill, much like a floating fence. Booms help to keep the oil in one place.

All booms share four features: 1) an above-water "freeboard," which helps prevent small waves from splashing oil over the top; 2) a below-water "skirt" to contain oil below the boom as much as possible; 3) a flotation device to keep the boom on the surface; and 4) an anchoring device, which keeps the booms and the oil they surround in one place.

Although some booms are designed especially for rough water, they work best in calm water where the surface is smooth and there's little current. Booms don't work at all when currents, wind, and waves are present—the booms bounce around, and waves wash the oil over and under them. Booms require constant tending and maintenance, and they need to be moved as the tides move the oil slick.

Equipment is not always immediately available when an oil spill occurs. The Environmental Protection Agency (EPA) stresses that containment is critical; people on the scene of a spill should use anything they can lay their hands on to keep the oil from spreading:

Improvised booms are made from such common materials as wood, plastic pipe, inflated fire hoses, automobile tires, and empty oil drums. They can be as simple as a board placed across the surface of a slow-moving stream, or a wall of sand built by bulldozers on a beach, to divert oil from a sensitive section of shoreline.

In 1989 booms helped to contain thousands of gallons of the oil spilling from the giant oil tanker *Exxon Valdez*. The water in Prince William Sound, Alaska, was exceptionally calm at the time of the spill, and workers were able to surround the damaged tanker with booms while they removed the remaining oil from the ship. Even so, as the full impact of the *Exxon Valdez* disaster demonstrates, booms are only part of the solution.

Skimmers

If the oil can be contained, the next task workers face is to get it out of the water. A skimmer is a device used to retrieve oil from the water's surface. Working somewhat like a household vacuum cleaner, skimmers can be used from shore or from a boat.

Boats equipped with mechanical skimmers can recover some of the oil from the boom-enclosed area and get it back into storage tanks. Like booms, skimmers work best in calm seas. In rough or choppy seas, skimmers suck up more water than oil. Skimmers also need to be constantly tended and cleaned since, in addition to oil, they also suck up any debris or ice that's in the water.

Sorbents

Sorbents, which are materials that soak up liquids, are another way of gathering up spilled oil. Cleanup workers spread them over the surface of an oil spill so that they soak up the oil. The sorbents are later gathered up, and the oil is squeezed out.

Burning

Burning is another tool used to clean up an oil spill. In burning, the oil is ignited on the surface of the water. Although no oil is recovered with this method, no oil is left to destroy beaches and the animals and plants that live in or near the polluted water.

Burning can only be done in open waters where there is no danger to other ships, drilling rigs, or the shoreline. A fire boom is placed around the spill to contain it during the burning. In addition to the dangers posed by the fire, air pollution is also a problem.

Helping biodegradation

Biological technologies are also used on oil spills. Some biological agents—certain chemicals and bacteria—will actually aid and increase the natural process of biodegradation, the breaking down of living materials into simpler and smaller parts.

Natural biodegradation of a large oil spill can take years, but when it comes to areas that have a sensitive ecology, this isn't fast enough. The addition of biological agents can speed up the biodegradation process and help reduce damage to water habitats.

Dispersants

Sometimes, as in the case of extremely light oils, a spill spreads too thinly to be contained. In those cases, instead of trying to retrieve the oil, cleanup workers do just the opposite: They try to disperse it, or scatter it in different directions.

Dispersants are chemicals that react with liquid substances, such as oil, and break them into tiny drops, similar to the way weathering naturally thins out and breaks up a spill. The smaller broken-down drops then mix with the water, and winds, waves, and currents break them down even further. Thus, dispersants help clear oil from the surface of the water, making it less likely that the oil slick will reach the shoreline. Often a dispersant is nothing more than a strong detergent, such as the kind used to wash laundry and dishes.

When oil hits a shoreline

The major concern of most cleanup workers is to keep an oil spill from reaching the shore, since shoreline environments are more sensitive and cleanup is more difficult. Unfortunately, despite efforts to contain and clean up an oil spill at sea, oil usually washes onto beaches. When this happens, even though cleanup operations with booms and skimmers continue in open water, other measures are needed. Physical methods, such as wiping with sorbent (sponge-like) materials, pressure washing, and raking and bulldozing are used to clean up shorelines.

Cleaning Up the Environment

The type of coastline an oil spill hits helps determine cleanup procedures. Sandy beaches require different approaches than rocky coastlines do; marshes require still other treatments.

Cleaning the cleanup materials

Once the spilled oil has been removed from the environment, there's still a lot of cleanup to be done. Anything that has oil on it needs to be cleaned, and this includes all the materials and equipment that were used to clean up the spill. Booms, skimmers, suction hoses, sorbent materials, and the protective clothing worn by workers—all have to be cleaned. Frequently, the sorbent materials and protective clothing have to be disposed of because they can't be cleaned.

Cleaning the cleanup materials poses its own set of problems. Any washing of materials creates produced water, or water that contains oil. This water needs to be either disposed of or recycled. Sorbent materials also need to be disposed of in a way that doesn't pollute the environment. Special waste sites need to be created since oil-covered materials can't just be deposited in the city dump.

The cleanup materials left over after an oil spill illustrate the main problem of such spills: Spilled oil is almost impossible to get rid of, and some of it will always remain in the environment.

Cleaning up the environment after an oil spill is only one part of the problem. Cleaning up all the wildlife and helping populations recover is another enormous task cleanup workers face.

Fard[1]

by Aldous Huxley

Some people refuse to look at other people's suffering.

They had been quarreling now for nearly an hour. Stooping over her sewing, Sophie wondered, without much curiosity, what it was all about this time. It was Madame's voice that she heard most often. Shrill with anger and indignant with tears, it burst out in gusts. Her husband was more self-controlled, and his deeper voice was too softly pitched to pass easily through the closed doors and to carry along the passage. To Sophie, in her cold little room, the quarrel sounded, most of the time, like a series of speeches by Madame, interrupted by strange silences.

After a time Sophie paid no more heed to the noise of quarreling. She was mending one of Madame's dresses, and the work required all her attention. She felt very tired; her body ached all over. It had been a hard day; so had yesterday, so had the

Reprinted by permission of Huxley Literary Estate. First appeared in *Young Archimedes* by Aldous Huxley. Copyright © 1924, 1952, by Aldous Huxley.

day before. Every day was a hard day, and she wasn't so young as she had been. Two years more and she'd be fifty. Every day had been a hard day since she could remember. She thought of the sacks of potatoes she used to carry when she was a little girl in the country. Slowly, slowly she was walking along the dusty road with the sack over her shoulder. Ten steps more; she could manage that. Only it never was the end; one always had to begin again.

She looked up from her sewing, moved her head from side to side, blinked. She had begun to see lights and spots of color dancing before her eyes; it often happened to her now. A sort of yellowish bright worm was moving up towards the right-hand corner of her field of vision. And there were stars of red and green that snapped and brightened and faded all round the worm. They moved between her and her sewing; they were there when she shut her eyes. After a moment she went on with her work; Madame wanted her dress most particularly tomorrow morning. But it was difficult to see round the worm.

There was suddenly a great increase of noise from the other end of the corridor. A door had opened; words spilled forth.

Madame's husband uttered a harsh, dangerous laugh. There was the sound of heavy footsteps in the passage; then the door banged.

Sophie looked down again at her work. Oh, the worm, the colored stars, the aching fatigue in all her limbs! If one could only spend a whole day in bed—in a huge bed, feathery, warm and soft, all the day long....

Fard   **111**

The ringing of the bell startled her. It always made her jump, that furious wasplike buzzer. Once more the bell buzzed furiously. Madame was impatient.

"At last, Sophie. I thought you were never coming."

Sophie said nothing; there was nothing to say. Madame was standing in front of the open wardrobe. Several dresses hung over her arm, and there were more of them lying in a heap on the bed. She was amazingly beautiful tonight. Her cheeks were flushed; her blue eyes shone with an unusual brilliance between their long lashes; her short, red-brown hair had broken wildly loose.

"Tomorrow, Sophie," she said dramatically, "we start for Rome. Tomorrow morning." She unhooked another dress from the wardrobe as she spoke, and threw it onto the bed. With the movement her dressing gown flew open, and there was a vision of fancy underclothing and white skin.

"We must pack at once."

"For how long, Madame?"

"The important thing is to get away. I shall not return to this house, after what has been said to me tonight, till I am humbly asked to."

"We had better take the large trunk, then, Madame; I will go and get it."

The air in the box-room was sickly with the smell of dust and leather. The big trunk was jammed in a far corner. She had to bend and strain at it in order to pull it out. The worm and the colored stars flickered before her eyes; she felt dizzy when she straightened herself. "I'll help you to pack, Sophie," said Madame, when the servant returned, dragging the heavy trunk after her. What a death's-head the old woman looked nowadays! She hated having old, ugly people near her. But Sophie was so efficient; it would be madness to get rid of her.

"Madame need not trouble." There would be no end to it, Sophie knew, if Madame started opening drawers and throwing things about. "Madame had much better go to bed. It's late."

Sophie began packing. A whole day in bed, in a huge, soft bed, like Madame's. One would doze, one would wake up for a moment, one would doze again.

"His latest game," Madame was saying angrily, "is to tell me he hasn't got any money. I'm not to buy any clothes, he says. I can't go about unclothed, can I?" She threw out her hands. "And as for saying he can't afford it, that's simply nonsense. He can, perfectly well. Only he's mean, mean, horribly mean. And if he'd only do a little honest work, for a change, instead of writing silly stories and publishing them at his own expense, he'd have plenty to spare." She walked up and down the room. "Besides," she went on, "there's his old father. What's he for, I should like to know? 'You must be proud of having a poet for a husband,' he says." She made her voice shake like an old man's. "It's all I can do not to laugh in his face. As for the love he talks so much about in his beastly stories," she laughed, "that's all pure invention. But, my good Sophie, what are you thinking of? Why are you packing that ugly old green dress?"

Sophie pulled out the dress without saying anything. Why did the woman choose this night to look so terribly ill? She had a yellow face and blue teeth. Madame shuddered; it was too horrible. She ought to send her to bed. But, after all, the work had to be done. What could one do about it?

"Life is terrible." Sighing, she sat down heavily on the edge of the bed. The bedsprings rocked her gently once or twice before they settled to rest. "To be married to a man like this. I shall soon be getting old and fat. And never once unfaithful. But look how he treats me." She got up again and began to wonder aimlessly about the room. "I won't stand it, though," she burst out. She had halted in front of the long mirror and was admiring her own wonderful figure. No one would believe, to look at her, that she was over thirty. Behind her she could see in the glass a thin, miserable, old creature, with a yellow face and blue teeth, crouching over the trunk. Really, it was too disagreeable. Sophie looked like one of those beggar women one sees on a cold morning, standing in the gutter. Does one hurry past, trying not to look at them? Or does one stop, open one's purse, and give them one's change? But whatever one did, one always felt uncomfortable, one always felt one had to apologize for one's furs. That was what came of walking. If one had a car—but that was another of her husband's meannesses—one wouldn't, rolling along behind closed windows, have to be aware of them at all. She turned away from the glass.

"I won't stand it," she said, trying not to think of the beggar woman, of blue teeth in a yellow face; "I won't stand it." She dropped into a chair.

But think of a lover with a yellow face and blue uneven teeth! She closed her eyes, shuddered at the thought. It would be enough to make one sick. She had to take another look: Sophie's eyes were the color of greenish lead, quite without life. What was one to do about it? And besides, the sight of it was making her feel positively ill.

Sophie rose slowly and with difficulty from her knees; an expression of pain crossed her face. Slowly she walked to the chest of drawers, slowly counted out six pairs of silk stockings. She turned back towards the trunk. The woman was a walking skeleton.

"Life is terrible," Madame repeated firmly. "Terrible, terrible, terrible."

She ought to send the woman to bed. But she would never be able to get her packing done by herself. And it was so important to get off tomorrow morning. She had told her husband she would go, and he had simply laughed; he hadn't believed it. She must give him a lesson this time. Perhaps . . . But she could think of nothing but Sophie's face; the leaden eyes, the bluish teeth, the yellow, wrinkled skin.

"Sophie," she said suddenly; it was with difficulty that she could prevent herself screaming, "look on my dressing table. You'll see a box of blush. Put a little on your cheeks. And there's some lipstick in the right-hand drawer."

She kept her eyes shut while Sophie got up—with what a horrible creaking of the joints!—walked over to the dressing table, and stood there, moving quietly through what seemed forever. What a life, my God, what a life! Slow footsteps trailed back again. She opened her eyes. Oh, that was far better, far better.

"Thank you, Sophie. You look much less tired now." She got up briskly. "And now we must hurry." Full of energy she ran to the wardrobe. "Goodness me," she exclaimed, throwing up her hands, "you've forgotten to put in my blue evening dress. How could you be so stupid, Sophie?"

---

¹ fard: a kind of makeup used on the face

The Most Dangerous GAME

PART ONE

by Richard Connell

The big-game hunter knew no fear. He was about to learn the meaning of terror.

"Off there to the right—somewhere—is a large island," said Whitney. "It's a mystery—"

"What island is it?" Rainsford asked.

"The old charts call it 'Ship-Trap Island,'" Whitney replied. "A suggestive name, isn't it? Sailors have a curious dread of the place. I don't know why. Some superstition—"

"Can't see it," remarked Rainsford, trying to peer through the damp tropical night as it pressed its thick warm blackness upon the yacht.

"You've good eyes," said Whitney, with a laugh, "and I've seen you pick off a moose moving in the brown fall bush at four hundred yards, but even you can't see four miles through a moonless Caribbean night."

"Not even four yards," admitted Rainsford. "Ugh! It's like moist black velvet."

"It will be light in Rio," promised Whitney. "We should make it in a few days. I hope the jaguar[1] guns have arrived. We should have some good hunting up the Amazon. Great sport, hunting."

"The best sport in the world," agreed Rainsford.

"For the hunter," said Whitney. "Not the jaguar."

"Don't talk rot, Whitney," said Rainsford. "You're a big-game hunter, not a philosopher. Who cares how a jaguar feels?"

"Perhaps a jaguar does," observed Whitney.

"Bah! They've no understanding."

"Even so, I think they understand one thing— fear. The fear of pain and the fear of death."

"Nonsense," laughed Rainsford. "This hot weather is making you soft, Whitney. The world is made up of two classes—the hunter and the hunted. Luckily, you and I are hunters. Do you think we've passed that island yet?"

"I can't tell in the dark. I hope so."

"Why?" asked Rainsford.

"The place has a reputation—a bad one."

"Cannibals?" suggested Rainsford.

"Hardly. Even those man-eating natives wouldn't live in such a place. But it's gotten into sailors' tales, somehow. Didn't you notice that the crew seemed very jumpy today?"

"They were a bit strange, now that you mention it. Even Captain Nielsen—"

"Yes, even that tough-minded old sailor, who'd go up to the devil and ask for a light. All I could get out of him was: 'This place has an evil name among sailors, sir.' Then he said to me, very gravely: 'Don't you feel anything?'—as if the air about us was actually poisonous. Now you mustn't laugh when I tell you this—I did feel something like a sudden chill.

"There was no breeze. The sea was as flat as glass. We were coming near the island then. What I felt was a—a mental chill, a sort of sudden dread."

"Pure imagination," said Rainsford. "One superstitious sailor can fill the whole ship's company with fear."

"Maybe. But sometimes I think sailors have an extra sense that tells them when they are in danger. Sometimes I think evil is almost touchable. Anyhow, I'm glad we're getting out of this zone. Well, I think I'll turn in now, Rainsford."

"I'm not sleepy," said Rainsford. "I'm going to smoke another pipe up on the deck."

"Good night, then, Rainsford. See you at breakfast."

"Right. Good night, Whitney."

There was no sound in the night as Rainsford sat there, but the muffled throb of the engine that drove the yacht swiftly through the darkness, and the swish and ripple of the wash of the propeller.

Rainsford, lying in a chair, lazily puffed on his favorite pipe. The drowsiness of the night was on him. "It's so dark," he thought, "that I could sleep without closing my eyes; the night would be my eyelids—"

A sudden sound startled him. Off to the right he heard it, and his ears, expert in such matters, could not be mistaken. Again he heard the sound, and again. Somewhere, off in the blackness, someone had fired a gun three times.

Rainsford sprang up and moved quickly to the rail. He strained his eyes in the direction from which the shots had come, but it was like trying to see through a blanket. He leaped upon the rail and balanced himself there, to see better; his pipe, hitting a rope, was knocked from his mouth. He lunged for it; a short, hoarse cry came from his lips as he realized he had reached too far and had lost his balance. The cry was pinched off short as the blood-warm waters of the Caribbean Sea closed over his head.

He struggled up to the surface and tried to cry out, but the wash from the speeding yacht slapped him in the face and the salt water in his mouth made him gag. Desperately he struck out with strong strokes after the disappearing lights of the yacht, but he stopped before he had swum fifty feet. A certain coolheadedness had come to him; it was not the first time he had been in a tight place. There was a chance that his cries could be heard by someone aboard the yacht, but that chance was slender, and grew more slender as the yacht raced on. He wrestled himself out of his clothes and shouted with all his power. The lights of the yacht were faint and vanishing fireflies; then they were blotted out entirely by the night.

Rainsford remembered the shots. They had come from the right, and with determination he swam in that direction, swimming with slow strokes, conserving his strength. For a seemingly endless time he

fought the sea. He began to count his strokes; he could do possibly a hundred more and then—

Rainsford heard a sound. It came out of the darkness, a high screaming sound, of a terrified animal in extreme pain.

He did not recognize the animal that made the sound; he did not try to. With new strength he swam toward the sound. He heard it again; then it was cut off by another noise, crisp, sharp.

"Pistol shot," Rainsford muttered, swimming on.

Ten minutes of determined effort brought another sound to his ears—the most welcome he had ever heard—the muttering and growling of the sea breaking on a rocky shore. He was almost on the rocks before he saw them; on a night less calm he would have been shattered against them. With his remaining strength he dragged himself from the swirling waters. Jagged crags appeared to jut up into the night; he forced himself upward, hand over hand. Gasping, his hands raw, he reached a flat place at the top. Dense jungle came down to the very edge of the cliffs. What perils that tangle of trees and bushes might hold for him did not concern Rainsford just then. All he knew was that he was safe from his enemy, the sea, and that total weariness was on him. He flung himself down at the jungle's edge and tumbled forward into the deepest sleep of his life.

When he opened his eyes he knew from the position of the sun that it was late afternoon. Sleep had given him vigor; a sharp hunger was picking at him. He looked about him, almost cheerfully.

"Where there are pistol shots, there are men. Where there are men, there is food," he thought. "But what kind of men," he wondered, "in so forbidding a place?" An unbroken front of snarled and ragged jungle fringed the shore.

He saw no sign of a trail through the closely knit web of weeds and trees; it was easier to go along the shore, and Rainsford stumbled along by the water. Not far from where he landed, he stopped.

Some wounded thing, by the evidence a large animal, had thrashed about in the bushes; the jungle weeds were crushed down and the moss was broken; one patch of weeds was stained red. A small glittering object not far away caught Rainsford's eye and he picked it up. It was an empty cartridge from a gun.

"A twenty-two," he remarked. "That's odd. It must have been a large animal, too. The hunter was brave to tackle it with such a small gun. It's clear that the beast put up a fight. I suppose the first three shots I heard were when the hunter flushed his quarry and wounded it. The last shot was when he trailed it here and finished it."

He examined the ground closely and found what he had hoped to find—the print of hunting boots. They pointed along the cliff in the direction he had been going. Eagerly he hurried along, now slipping on a rotten log or loose stone, but making good time; night was beginning to settle down on the island.

Night was blacking out the sea and jungle when Rainsford sighted the lights. He came upon them as he turned a corner in the coastline, and his first thought was that he had come upon a village, for there were many lights. But as he forged along, he saw to his great astonishment that all the lights were in one enormous building—a lofty structure with pointed towers plunging upward into the gloom. It was set on a high bluff, and on three sides of it cliffs dived down to where the sea licked greedy lips in the shadows.

"Like a dream," thought Rainsford. But it was no dream, he found, when he opened the tall spiked iron gate. The stone steps were real enough; the huge door was real enough; yet all about it hung a dreamlike air.

He knocked at the door and was surprised by the booming loudness. He thought he heard steps within; the door remained closed. Again Rainsford knocked. The door opened then, as suddenly as if it were on a spring, and Rainsford stood blinking in the river of glaring gold light that poured out. The first thing Rainsford's eyes beheld was the largest man Rainsford had ever seen—a gigantic creature, solidly made and black-bearded to the waist. In his hand the man held a long-barreled revolver, and he was pointing it straight at Rainsford's heart.

End of part 1

---

[1] jaguar: the largest of the wild cats that live in South America

The Most Dangerous

GAME

PART TWO

by Richard Connell

He loved to hunt, but there are limits to what a man will kill.

"Don't be alarmed," said Rainsford, with a smile. "I'm no robber. I fell off a yacht. My name is Sanger Rainsford of New York City."

The menacing look in the eyes did not change. The revolver pointed as rigidly as if the giant man were a statue. He gave no sign that he understood Rainsford's words, or that he had even heard them. He was dressed in a black uniform trimmed with gray.

"I'm Sanger Rainsford of New York," Rainsford began again. "I fell off a yacht. I am hungry."

The man's only answer was to raise with his thumb the hammer of his revolver. Then Rainsford saw the man's free hand go to his forehead in a salute, and he saw him click his heels together and stand at attention. Another man was coming down the broad steps, an erect, slender man in evening clothes. He advanced to Rainsford and held out his hand.

"It is a great pleasure and honor to welcome Mr. Sanger Rainsford, the celebrated hunter, to my home," the man said with a slight accent.

Rainsford shook the man's hand.

"I've read your book about hunting in Tibet, you see," explained the man. "I am General Zaroff."

Rainsford's first impression was that the man was very handsome; his second was that there was an original, almost strange quality about his face. He was a tall man, past middle age. His hair was a vivid white, but his thick eyebrows and pointed mustache were black. His eyes, too, were black and very bright. Turning to the giant in uniform, the general made a sign. The giant put away his pistol, saluted, and went.

"Ivan is a very strong fellow," remarked the general, "but he has the misfortune to be deaf and dumb. A simple fellow, but, I'm afraid, a bit savage.

"Come," he said, "we shouldn't be chatting here. We can talk later. Now you want clothes, food, and rest. You shall have them. This is a most restful spot."

Ivan reappeared, and the general spoke to him with lips that moved but made no sound.

"Follow Ivan, Mr. Rainsford," said the general. "I was about to have my dinner when you came. I'll wait for you. You'll find that my clothes will fit you, I think."

Ivan led him to a big bedroom with a huge bed. Rainsford changed into a suit that, he noticed, was made in London.

The dining room that Rainsford was shown into was remarkable. There was a royal magnificence about it. It had high ceilings and a long table where twenty men could sit to eat. On the walls were mounted heads of many animals—lions, tigers, elephants, moose, bears; larger and more perfect specimens Rainsford had never seen. At the great table the general was sitting, alone.

"Would you like a drink, Mr. Rainsford?" he asked. The drink was very good; and, Rainsford noted, everything on the table was the finest money could buy.

They were eating borsch, the rich red soup with sour cream so dear to the Russians. "We do our best to preserve a civilized life here. Please forgive me if there is anything missing. We are off the beaten track, you know. Do you think the wine has suffered from its long ocean trip?"

"Not in the least," declared Rainsford. He was finding the general a very good host. But there was one thing that made him uncomfortable. Whenever he looked up from his plate he found the general studying him carefully.

"Perhaps," said General Zaroff, "you were surprised that I recognized your name. You see, I read all books on hunting. I've but one love in my life, Mr. Rainsford, and it is the hunt."

"You have some wonderful heads here," said Rainsford as he ate a delicious steak. "That buffalo is the largest I ever saw."

"Oh, that fellow. Yes, he was a monster."

"Did he attack you?"

"Hurled me against a tree," said the general. "Cracked my skull. But I got the beast."

"I've always thought," said Rainsford, "that the buffalo is the most dangerous of all big game."

The general was quiet for a moment; he was smiling a curious red-lipped smile. Then he said slowly: "No, you are wrong, sir."

"What do you mean?" Rainsford asked.

"I've invented a new animal."

"A new animal? You're joking."

"Not at all," said the general. "I never joke about hunting. I was growing bored. Hunting had become too easy; I always got my quarry. I needed a new animal; I found one. I bought this island, built this house, and here I do my hunting. This island is perfect for my purposes—there are jungles with trails, hills, swamps—"

"But the animal?"

"Oh," said the general, "it supplies me with the most exciting hunting in the world. No other hunting compares with it. Every day I hunt, and I never grow bored, for now I have a quarry with which I can match wits."

Rainsford's confusion showed in his face.

"I wanted the ideal animal to hunt," explained the general. "So I said: 'What makes the ideal quarry?' And the answer was: 'It must have courage, cunning, and, above all, it must be able to reason.'"

"But no animal can reason," objected Rainsford.

"My dear fellow," the general said, "there is one that can."

"But you can't mean—" gasped Rainsford.

"And why not?"

"I can't believe you are serious, General Zaroff. This is an ugly joke."

"Why should I not be serious? I am speaking of hunting."

"Hunting, General Zaroff? What you speak of is killing other men."

The general laughed with good nature. "I refuse to believe that so modern and civilized a young man as you has such romantic ideas about the value of human life."

The Most Dangerous Game, part 2   **129**

"I'm not a cold-blooded killer," said Rainsford.

"I bet you'll forget your high notions when you go hunting with me. You've a great new thrill in store for you, Mr. Rainsford."

"No thank you, General Zaroff, I'm a hunter, not a man-killer."

"Life is for the strong, to be lived by the strong, and, if need be, taken by the strong. The weak of the world were put here to give the strong pleasure. I am strong. Why should I not use my gift? If I wish to hunt, why should I not? I hunt the garbage of the earth—sailors from tramp ships—a horse or hound is worth more than all of them."

"But they are men," said Rainsford hotly.

"Exactly," said the general. "That is why I use them. It gives me pleasure. They can reason, after a fashion. So they are dangerous."

"But where do you get them?"

"This island is called Ship-Trap," he answered. "Sometimes the high seas get angry and send them to me. Sometimes, I help the seas a bit. Come to the window."

Rainsford went to the window and looked out toward the sea.

"Watch! Out there!" exclaimed the general, pointing into the night. Rainsford saw only blackness, and then, as the general pressed a button, far out to sea Rainsford saw the flash of lights.

The general chuckled. "They indicate a channel," he said, "where there's none; giant rocks with very sharp edges wait under the water like a sea monster. They can crush a ship as easily as I crush this nut."

He dropped a walnut on the hardwood floor and brought his heel grinding down on it.

"Now we'll visit my training school," smiled the general. "It's in the cellar. I have about a dozen students down there. They're from a Spanish ship that had some trouble on the rocks."

"But what if they refuse to be hunted? What do you do then?"

"Oh," said the general, "I give them a choice, of course. They don't have to play that game if they don't want to. If they do not wish to hunt, I turn them over to Ivan. Mr. Rainsford, they always choose the hunt."

"And if they win?"

A smile appeared on the general's face. "I have not lost—yet," he said.

"I hope," said Rainsford, "that you will excuse me tonight, General Zaroff. I'm really not feeling at all well."

"Well, I suppose that's only natural, after your long swim. You need a good night's sleep. Tomorrow you'll feel like a new man. Then we'll hunt."

Rainsford was hurrying from the room.

"Sorry you can't come with me tonight," called the general. "I expect some good hunting. I'm after a big, strong man. Well, good night, Mr. Rainsford."

Rainsford went to bed. He tried to sleep but could not. Once he thought he heard footsteps outside his door. He tried to throw open the door; it was locked. He went back to the bed and lay down. As he finally started to doze off, he heard, far off in the jungle, a pistol shot.

General Zaroff didn't appear until lunch. "I don't feel so well," he said to Rainsford. "The hunt was not good last night. The fellow lost his head. He offered no problems at all. I am worried. I feel the return of my boredom with the hunt."

"General," said Rainsford, "I wish to leave this island at once."

"But my dear fellow," protested the general, "you've only just arrived. You've had no hunting. Tonight we will hunt—you and I."

"No, general," Rainsford said, "I will not hunt."

"As you wish, my friend," he said. "But may I suggest that you'll find my idea of sport more diverting than Ivan's?"

"You don't mean—"

"You'll find the game worth playing," the general said. "Your brain against mine. Your strength against mine."

The general sipped his wine. "Well, I must beg your pardon, I always take a nap after lunch. You'll hardly have time for a nap, Mr. Rainsford. You'll want to start, I guess. I won't follow until dusk. Hunting at night is so much more exciting than by day, don't you think? Good-bye, Mr. Rainsford."

General Zaroff strolled from the room.

From another door came Ivan. Under one arm he carried hunting clothes, a sack of food, and a hunting knife, which he handed to Rainsford. His right hand rested on a gun thrust in his belt.

The game began.

End of part 2

The Most Dangerous
GAME
PART THREE

by Richard Connell

Who will win this deadly game: the hunter or the hunted?

Rainsford had fought his way through the bush for two hours. "I must keep my nerve," he said.

His whole idea at first was to put distance between himself and General Zaroff, and, to this end, he had plunged along. Now he had got a grip on himself, had stopped, and was taking stock of the situation.

He saw that straight flight was useless; sooner or later it would bring him to the sea.

"I'll give him a trail to follow," muttered Rainsford, and he struck off from the path he had been following into the trackless jungle. He doubled on his trail again and again. Night found him tired, with hands and face lashed by branches. He knew it would be insane to blunder on through the dark, even if he had the strength. His need for rest was most important. A big tree with a thick trunk and outspread branches was nearby, and taking care to leave not the slightest mark, he climbed up into the branches. He stretched out on one of its broad limbs and rested. Even a hunter like the general could not trace him here, he told himself; only the devil himself could follow that complicated trail through the jungle after dark. But, perhaps, the general was a devil—

Night crawled by slowly, and sleep did not visit Rainsford. The jungle was silent. Toward morning, as the sky was washed with gray, the cry of some startled bird focused Rainsford's attention in that direction. Something was coming through the bush, coming slowly, carefully, coming by the same winding way Rainsford had come. He flattened himself down on the limb, and through a screen of leaves, he watched. The thing coming was a man.

It was General Zaroff. He made his way along with his eyes fixed in concentration on the ground before him. He paused, almost beneath the tree, dropped to his knees, and studied the ground. Rainsford's impulse was to hurl himself down like a lion, but he saw that the general's right hand held a small pistol.

The hunter shook his head several times, as if he were puzzled. Then he straightened up and took from his case one of his cigarettes; its smoke drifted up to Rainsford's nostrils.

Rainsford held his breath. The general's eyes had left the ground and were traveling inch by inch up the tree. Rainsford froze there, every muscle tensed for a spring. But the sharp eyes of the hunter stopped before they reached the limb where Rainsford lay; a smile spread over his brown face. He blew a smoke ring into the air; then he turned his back on the tree and walked carelessly away, back along the trail he had come.

The air burst hotly from Rainsford's lungs. His first thought made him feel sick and numb. The general could follow a trail through the woods at night; he must have great powers; only by the merest chance had he failed to see his quarry.

Rainsford's second thought was even more terrible. It sent a shudder of cold horror through his whole being. Why had the general smiled? Why had he turned back?

Rainsford did not want to believe what his reason told him was true, but the truth was evident. The general was playing with him! The general was saving him for another day's sport!

"I will not lose my nerve. I will not."

He slid down from the tree and struck off again into the woods. He forced his mind to work. Three hundred yards from his hiding place he stopped where a huge dead tree leaned on a smaller, living one. Throwing off his sack of food, Rainsford took his knife and began to work with all his energy.

The job was finished at last, and he threw himself down behind a fallen log a hundred feet away. He did not have to wait long. The cat was coming again to play with the mouse.

Following the trail with the sureness of a bloodhound, came General Zaroff. Nothing escaped those searching black eyes, no crushed blade of grass, no bent twig, no mark, no matter how small. General

Zaroff was concentrating so hard on following the trail that he was upon the thing Rainsford had made before he saw it. His foot touched the branch that was the trigger. Even as he touched it, the general sensed his danger and leaped back with the grace of a cat. But he was not quite quick enough; the dead tree crashed down and struck the general a blow on the shoulder, and Rainsford, with fear again gripping his heart, heard the general's laugh ring through the jungle.

"Rainsford," called the general, "if you are within sound of my voice, as I suppose you are, let me congratulate you. Not many men know how to make a Malay man-catcher. You are proving interesting, Mr. Rainsford. I'll be back."

When the general, rubbing his shoulder, had gone, Rainsford took up his flight again. It was flight now, a desperate, hopeless flight that carried him on for hours. Dusk came, then darkness, and still he pressed on. The ground grew softer under his feet; the trees grew denser; insects bit him savagely. Then, as he stepped forward, his foot sank into the ooze. He tried to pull it out, but the mud sucked at his foot as if it were a giant vacuum. With a violent effort, he tore his foot loose.

The softness of the earth gave him an idea. He stepped back from the mud and began to dig.

The pit grew deeper; when it was above his shoulders, Rainsford climbed out and from some hard small trees he cut stakes and sharpened them to a fine point. He planted the stakes in the bottom of the pit with the points sticking up. With flying fingers he wove a rough carpet of weeds and branches and with

it covered the mouth of the pit. Then he crouched behind the stump of a fallen tree.

He knew his hunter was coming; he heard the sound of feet on the soft earth, and the night breeze brought him the smoke of the general's cigarette. Rainsford could not see the general or the pit. Then he felt an urge to cry aloud for joy, for he heard the sharp crackle of the breaking branches as the cover of the pit gave way; he heard the sharp scream of pain as the pointed stakes found their mark. He leaped up. Then he hid again. Three feet from the pit a man was standing with lantern.

"You've done well, Rainsford," the voice of the general called. "Your pit has claimed one of my best dogs. Again you score. I'll see what you can do against my whole pack. I'm going home for a rest now. Thank you for a most amusing evening."

At daybreak Rainsford was awakened by a sound that made him know he had new things to learn about fear. It was a distant sound, but he knew it. It was the howling of a pack of hounds.

Rainsford knew he could do one of two things. He could stay where he was and wait. That was sure death. He could flee. That would only delay death a short time. For a moment he stood there, thinking. An idea that held a wild chance came to him. He headed away from the swamp.

The howling of the hounds drew nearer. On a ridge Rainsford climbed a tree. Not a quarter of a mile away, he could see the bushes moving. He saw the lean figure of General Zaroff. Just in front of the general he could see Ivan being pulled by the dogs.

They would be on him any minute now. He slid down the tree. He caught hold of a young tree and to it he fastened his hunting knife, with the blade pointing down the trail; with a bit of vine he tied back the tree. Then he ran for his life.

When he stopped to get his breath, he heard the howling of the hounds stop. They must have reached the knife.

He climbed up a tree and looked back. He saw with terror that the general was still on his feet. But Ivan was not. The knife had not totally failed.

Rainsford had hardly tumbled to the ground when the pack took up the cry again.

The sea showed between the trees ahead. Ever nearer drew the hounds. Rainsford forced himself on.

Across a cove he could see the general's house. Twenty feet below him the sea rumbled and hissed. He heard the dogs. Then he leaped far out into water…

When the general and his dogs reached the beach, they stopped. For some minutes he stood regarding the blue-green sea. He shrugged his shoulders.

General Zaroff had a good dinner that evening. Two slight annoyances, however, kept him from perfect enjoyment. One was the thought that it would be difficult to replace Ivan; the other was that his quarry had escaped. At ten he went up to his bedroom. He was very tired. There was a little moonlight, so, before turning on the light, he went to the window and looked down at the courtyard. He could see the hounds. Then he switched on the light.

A man stepped out from behind the curtains.

"Rainsford!" screamed the general. "How in God's name did you get here?"

"Swam," said Rainsford. "I found it quicker than walking through the jungle."

The general sucked in his breath and smiled. "I congratulate you," he said. "You have won the game."

Rainsford did not smile. "I am still the hunted," he said. "Get ready, General Zaroff."

The general bowed. "I see," he said. "Splendid! One of us is to furnish a meal for the dogs. The other will sleep in this most excellent bed."

He had never slept in a better bed, Rainsford decided.